CULTURES OF THE WORLD
Bhutan

Robert Cooper and Yong Jui Lin

mc **Marshall Cavendish**
Benchmark
New York

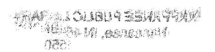

PICTURE CREDITS

Cover: © Ann Manner / Photodisc / Getty Images
alt.type / Reuters: 66 • Audrius Tomonis: 138 • Corbis: 12, 113, 122, 131 • Getty Images: 27, 29, 32, 33, 39, 77, 79, 91, 92, 110 • Hutchison Library: 67, 84 • John R. Jones: 24 • Lonely Planet Images: 13, 64, 71, 73, 95, 105, 25 • North Wind Pictures Archives: 25 • Photolibrary: 1, 3, 5, 6, 7, 8, 9, 10, 11, 14, 15, 16, 17, 18, 19, 20, 21, 22, 28, 30, 34, 35, 36, 37, 38, 40, 41, 42, 43, 44, 45, 46, 48, 49, 51, 52, 55, 56, 57, 59, 60, 61, 62, 63, 65, 69, 70, 74, 75, 78, 80, 81, 82, 85, 86, 89, 90, 94, 96, 97, 98, 99, 100, 101, 102, 103, 104, 106, 107, 108, 109, 111, 112, 115, 116, 119, 120, 121, 123, 124, 126, 127, 128, 129, 130

PRECEDING PAGE

A Buddhist *dzong* (monastery) is nestled within the Himalaya Mountains in Tongsa.

Publisher (U.S.): Michelle Bisson
Editors: Deborah Grahame-Smith, Peter Mavrikis, Mindy Pang
Copyreader: Daphne Hougham
Designers: Nancy Sabato, Lynn Chin
Cover picture researcher: Tracey Engel
Picture researcher: Joshua Ang

Marshall Cavendish Benchmark
99 White Plains Road
Tarrytown, NY 10591
Website: www.marshallcavendish.us

Originated and designed by Times Media Private Limited
An imprint of Marshall Cavendish International (Asia) Private Limited
A member of Times Publishing Limited

Marshall Cavendish is a trademark of Times Publishing Limited.

All Internet sites were correct and accurate at the time of printing. All monetary figures in this publication are in U.S. dollars.

Library of Congress Cataloging-in-Publication Data
Cooper, Robert, 1945 Aug. 2-
  Bhutan / Robert Cooper and Yong Jui Lin. — 2nd ed.
    p. cm. — (Cultures of the world)
  Includes bibliographical references and index.
  Summary: "Provides comprehensive information on the geography, history,
    wildlife, governmental structure, economy, cultural diversity, peoples,
    religion, and culture of Bhutan"—Provided by publisher.
  ISBN 978-1-60870-453-8
  1. Bhutan—Juvenile literature. I. Yong, Jui Lin. II. Title.
  DS491.4.C66 2011
    954.98—dc22   2010042565

Printed in China
7 6 5 4 3 2 1

CONTENTS

INTRODUCTION

THE KINGDOM OF BHUTAN IS A SMALL, LANDLOCKED COUNTRY situated between Tibet in the north and west and India in the east (Assam), the south (West Bengal), and in the west (Sikkim). With an area of 13,285 square miles (38,394 square kilometers), Bhutan shares a latitude with southern Florida but is considerably colder because of its location in the Himalayas—the "Roof of the World." Bhutan is one of the most ruggedly mountainous countries in the world, rising from a narrow semitropical strip on the southern border to over 24,835 feet (7,570 meters) in the north. Home to some 750,000 people (2010 estimate), it is a land of soaring snowcapped peaks, alpine meadows, and densely forested hills. Until the 1960s, this Buddhist kingdom existed in self-imposed isolation. Developments, including direct international flights, the Internet, mobile phone networks, and cable television, have increasingly modernized the urban areas of the country. Bhutan has balanced such updating with its ancient culture and traditions under the guiding philosophy of gross national happiness (GNH). Bhutan's development strategy is extremely mindful of the need to nurture its rich environment. The government takes great measures to preserve the nation's traditional culture, identity, and the environment.

GEOGRAPHY

Snowcapped Mount Chomo Lhari in Paro looms over the serene village lying at its feet.

BHUTAN MEASURES ROUGHLY 93 miles (150 km) north to south and 186 miles (300 km) east to west. Apart from a southern strip that is barely 328 feet (100 m) above sea level, the country lies mostly in the glacier-covered Himalayan heights, rising to an elevation of 24,835 feet (7,570 m) in the north at Kangkar Puenzum Mountain.

Farmlands in Nobding. Despite its pocketbook size, Bhutan is a land of great diversity, with dense jungles, valleys, alpine highlands, and towering snow peaks side by side.

Bhutan controls several strategic mountain passes through the Himalayas, allowing travel between Tibet and Assam, a state in India. These passes are also the only way into the kingdom. Coupled with its centuries-old policies of isolationism, Bhutan has been called the Mountain Fortress of the Gods.

The climate in Bhutan varies with height (elevation), from subtropical in the south to temperate in the highlands to polar-type climate, clad with year-round snow, in the north. Bhutan has five distinguishable seasons: summer, monsoon, fall, winter, and spring. Western Bhutan has the heavier monsoon rains; southern Bhutan has hot humid summers and cool winters; central and eastern Bhutan is temperate and drier than the west with warm summers and cool winters. Moreover, regional climates can vary between valleys. The main rivers are usually deeply incised, and despite high rainfall throughout the country, agriculture is limited to areas closer to perennial streams.

Towering mountains and winding rivers sculpt the breathtaking landscape of Bhutan.

Centuries of isolation have preserved Bhutan's forests and abundant flora and fauna that, like so much about Bhutan, remain as they always were—untouched and beautiful.

PHYSICAL ENVIRONMENT

Being largely mountainous, Bhutan is markedly comparable to Switzerland both in its size and topography. Corresponding to a giant staircase, Bhutan's topography rises steadily from a narrow strip of land in the south to some of the highest unclimbed Himalayan peaks in the north—from the semitropical low-lying flatlands of the southern Duars (DOO-ars) to the valleys of the Central Himalayas at 3,282 to 9,846 feet (1,000—3,000 m), before giving way to the Great Himalaya Range, which soars high above 22,974 feet (7,000 m) along the Tibetan border.

Mountain chains averaging 9,800 feet (2,987 m) also run north to south from the Great Himalaya Range, physically isolating Bhutan's administrative regions in the western, central, and eastern parts of the country and greatly hindering attempts to improve interregional communications. Weather is extreme in the mountains: the high peaks have perpetual snow, and the lesser mountains and time-hewn gorges have year-round high winds, making them

barren brown wind tunnels in summer, and frozen wastelands in winter. These clean physical divisions closely mirror the ethnic divisions in Bhutan. As well, they influence the type of crops people grow, their diets, the flora and fauna that surround them, the languages they speak, and even their politics.

Rice terraces are carefully built along the fertile Paro Valley.

THE SOUTHERN DUARS

South of the Central Himalayan valleys and foothills unrolls the narrow Duars Plain, which forms a strip 8 to 10 miles (13—16 km) wide along the southern border of Bhutan. The Duars Plain provides the greatest expanse of fertile flatlands and is the wealthiest and most densely inhabited part of the country today. Only 8 percent of Bhutan is arable land, and most of it lies in the Duars area and in the river valleys leading from it.

Where the land is not tilled by farmers, it quickly becomes tropical savannah and forest. In recent decades dams have been constructed to provide hydroelectricity, and large towns, more Indian in style than Bhutanese, have grown up along the border.

The 18 valleys of the Duars act as natural portals into a country that is composed almost entirely of mountains. This characteristic gave the region its name, which shares a derivation with the English word "doors."

THE GREAT HIMALAYA RANGE

The northern part of Bhutan forms part of the Great Himalaya Range, which radiates south into the Central Himalayas. The snowcapped Himalayan Range reaches heights of over 29,035 feet (8,850 m) and extends along the Bhutan-China border.

Historically, communication with Tibet in the north has been more important than with India in the south. Although the Great Himalaya Range divides Bhutan and Tibet and covers 20 percent of Bhutan in perpetual snow, there are four *la* (LAH) or mountain passes linking the two countries. These *la* follow the course of rivers that over millennia have cut their beds deeply into the rock and earth, crossing into Bhutan at altitudes significantly lower than the mountain peaks. As a result, at certain times of the year, it was easier and safer to travel to Tibet than to India.

The jagged peaks support no life except, perhaps, that of the gods, as the Bhutanese believe. The people treat the Himalayas with great respect, and some peaks are considered sacred. Since passage to Tibet is always through mountain passes, some of which remain open all winter, the Bhutanese have no reason to climb the peaks. These passes are also the only way into the kingdom, and coupled with its centuries-old policy of national isolation, Bhutan has been called the Mountain Fortress of the Gods. The heartland of Bhutan has never been successfully invaded.

Bhutan is strategically located between China and India, controlling several key Himalayan mountain passes. This view is from the Dochu La Pass.

RIVERS

Rivers are an important source of electricity and revenue for Bhutan. Due to enormous deposits of snow and rain and a wide variation in altitude, Bhutan has a great potential for hydroelectric power. Only a few dams have been built, however. Since domestic needs are modest, most of the electrical energy produced is sold to India, underscoring its enormous value.

There are four main river systems running from west to east in Bhutan—the Manas, the Mo Chu or Sankosh, the Wong Chu or Raidak, and the Amo Chu or Torsa. Fed by glaciers, all the rivers are perennial and swell during the monsoon months. All of them originate in the Himalayas, with several entering Bhutan from Tibet. The Manas, which follows a circuitous route in the west of the country, is often cited as Bhutan's longest river with a total length of 1,988 miles (3,200 km).

Bhutan's rivers have many rapids and waterfalls, constantly fed by the tremendous amount of rain Bhutan receives every year. As a result, none of the rivers is navigable. Their waters carry vital nutrients from the glacial Himalayas and deposit them in the fertile lands of the upper-central valleys and the southern lowlands before crossing the Duars Plain and coursing into India, where they eventually join the Brahmaputra River.

Glacial lakes have been forming rapidly on the surfaces of glaciers in this region during the last few decades because of global warming.

The blue poppy was once thought to be mythical, like the yeti—its existence was much talked about but not verified. It was discovered in 1922 by the legendary mountaineer George Leigh Mallory. It remains extremely rare, growing only above the timberline at an elevation of around 11,483 feet to 14,764 feet (3,500–4,500 m). Known in the national language of Bhutan as euitgel metog hoem (AYT-gel meyt-og hoaym), the blue poppy—not a true poppy, just poppylike—a perennial, has a life span of three to five years. It grows up to 5 feet (1.5 m) tall, blooms only once at the beginning of the rains, produces seeds, dies, then regrows at the next rains.

CLIMATE

Primarily because of variations in altitude, Bhutan's climate differs greatly among regions, more so than in any other similarly sized area in the world. Three principal climatic regions can be identified in Bhutan—humid and subtropical in the southern plains, temperate climate with cool winters and hot summers in the central valleys, and severe winters and cool summers in the Himalayas. April and May are mostly windy with occasional showers. Strong gusts of wind arrive most afternoons, raising clouds of dust and shaking the roofs of simple houses.

Like most of Asia, Bhutan experiences monsoon rains. The summer monsoon, which lasts from June to late September, brings heavy rain from the southwest. As the monsoon sets in, days can pass with hardly a letup in the downpour. A rhythm soon develops, however, with most of the rain falling in the evenings and at night.

FLORA

The dramatic changes in altitude and climate in this country have resulted in a lush array of flora. Centuries of abstention from outside relations, a small population, and topographical extremes have led to Bhutan's maintaining one of the most intact ecosystems in the world. The country ranks among the top 10 countries in the world in terms of species density (species richness per unit area). Within a distance of only 62 miles (100 km), the rice paddies and fruit orchards of the south give way successively to deciduous forests then alpine forests, arriving finally at grassy meadows and fields of barley and winter wheat set among the mountains.

Houses seem to huddle together for warmth in the village of Laya, Gasa. In the highest mountain regions, even the rivers are permanently frozen into glaciers.

Bhutan has been called a botanical paradise. An astonishing variety of plants grow in Bhutan: over 5,400 species, including the edelweiss, the blue poppy (Bhutan's national flower), carnivorous plants, almost every type of orchid, giant rhubarb, and magnolia. These figures also include 300 species of locally grown medicinal plants, which has the country nicknamed the Land of Medicinal Plants. Of the more than 600 species of orchids too, most are commonly found on heights up to 6,890 feet (2,100 m), although some hardy species thrive even above 12,139 feet (3,700 m).

Tropical evergreen forests growing below 2,625 feet (800 m) are repositories of unique biodiversity. The next vegetation zone is the subtropical grasslands and forests found between 2,953 feet and 5,906 feet (900 m and 1,800 m). The tree rhododendron is found in this zone, along with forests of oak, walnut, and sal, or shala—a tree native to southern Asia. The temperate zone has forests of oak, birch, maple, magnolia, and laurel. Above 7,874 feet (2,400 m) live spruce, yew, and weeping cypress, and growing up to the tree line is the east Himalayan fir. Between the tree line and the snow line, at about 18,045 feet (5,500 m), are low shrubs, rhododendrons, Himalayan grasses, and flowering herbs. Blue poppy grows above the tree line and can be found atop some high passes from the far eastern parts of the country all the way across to the west.

A boreal forest, with its characteristic coniferous trees thriving in northern Bhutan.

FORESTS

At altitudes below 3,000 feet (914 m)—in the south and the Duars valleys extending into Bhutan—the forests are tropical. The most valuable forests in Bhutan are located between 3,282 to 9,846 feet (1,000—3,000 m), where cypress, fir, spruce, and juniper are found.

Until the beginning of the 20th century, the tropical forests formed a much needed barrier to the south, which contained two feared creatures— the tiger and the malarial mosquito. To the Bhutanese, who were used to higher, cooler climates where mosquitoes cannot survive, the lowlands were a menacing disease zone that had to be crossed to get to their southern neighbors.

The Bhutanese were uninterested in exploiting their forest resources and were happy to lease large tracts in the south to Assam, India. Forest cover gradually shrank back from Bhutan's western borders as immigrants from neighboring Nepal arrived throughout the first half of the 20th century, cut down the forests to clear the land, planted rice and orchard crops in the new fields, and built the still existing small border towns.

Bhutanese, who had little use for the land, welcomed the immigrants and encouraged migration by providing free land grants and economic assistance. The inescapable result was that Bhutan had more people, more marketable produce, but fewer trees.

About 72 percent of Bhutan is still under forest cover, and over 28 percent of the country is designated as protected area.

Until roads were built to the south in the 1960s, everybody was content with the situation. Bhutanese had no way of transporting any forest harvest and therefore did not seek control of the forests until well into the 20th century. Fortunately, the young king has led the government in a major effort to protect the forests.

The Royal Society for the Protection of Nature is a citizen-based nonprofit environmental organization that was established in 1986 to raise national awareness on environmental conservation and sustainable development throughout the country. A trust fund was set up in 1991 with money provided by the World Wildlife Fund and several European governments to assist in Bhutan's conservation efforts. The system of national parks was rapidly expanded, protected forest areas were increased, and forestry education was greatly extended.

It is still too early to evaluate the success of conservation programs, which face two major hurdles. The first, called slash-and-burn farming, is the timeworn method of farming, especially in the east, involving the cutting down of trees and setting them ablaze, then planting in the ashes. The other conservation hurdle is the reliance of most Bhutanese on firewood as cooking and heating fuel.

To reduce these problems, efforts have begun to provide alternative fuels, at least in the urban areas, and to teach responsible and efficient gathering of firewood. Education and fertilizer are said to be the twin tools for converting traditional farming methods into more forest-friendly systems. Also, a harder line has been drawn against tree poaching, and the transportation of trees and forest products into India is now closely controlled.

Commercial logging is controlled, and oak, pine, and tropical hardwoods are the valuable species most harvested.

These endangered birds migrate from Siberia and Tibet in mid-October to specific valleys in Bhutan, returning home when spring arrives. They are very much part of the local folklore, and Bhutanese who live in those areas hosting the 300 to 400 birds believe that they bring good luck. The Royal Society for the Protection of Nature has

introduced a Black-Necked Crane Festival, first held in November 1998. It was so popular with Bhutanese and foreigners that it has now become an annual event in the Phobjikha Valley.

FAUNA

The fauna of Bhutan is as diverse as its flora. The World Wildlife Fund recorded 165 species of mammals there, including many rare animals such as the golden langur, snow leopard, and red panda. Like the flora and the human population, different species of animals tend to prefer different habitats.

The southern forests are home to elephants, tigers, rhinoceroses, wild buffalo, countless snakes, and several species of monkey, including the golden langur, a small primate discovered only in the 20th century and believed to live only in southern Bhutan.

The Central Himalayas host black bears, red pandas, hornbills, wild boars, and the famous black-necked cranes, a rarity among the 770 species of birds recorded in Bhutan.

Northern areas above the tree line and the high valleys are the habitats of yaks, blue sheep, mountain goats, and Bhutan's national animal, the takin, a migratory ruminant that looks as if it has a cow's body and a sheep's head. This is also the home of the extremely rare and reclusive snow leopard, whose beautiful coat has resulted in overhunting, but at least leading to strict conservation measures.

In 1995 the Bhutan National Assembly ruled that at least 60 percent of the country must remain under permanent forest cover.

CITIES

More than 60 percent of Bhutanese live in small scattered villages and rely on agriculture and raising livestock for their livelihood. They come to town for free medical services, to go to market, and increasingly, to get an education. Very few, however, aspire to live in the kind of urban sprawl that exists on the other side of the southern frontier.

Urban settlements did not exist until the 1960s. They quietly arose following the construction of roads and economic development. Bhutan's capital, Thimphu, lies in a beautiful wooded valley and is the largest urban area in Bhutan, with a population of some 98,676 in the entire region (2005 estimate). There is only one main road, and while some of the new buildings are less than inspiring, traditional architecture predominates.

Phuntsholing, Bhutan's second-largest city, has a population of 21,000 and is accessible only by road. Cross-border trade has resulted in a thriving local economy, and the city serves as headquarters for the Bank of Bhutan. Punakha is the former capital city of Bhutan. Punakha Dzong is the most historic and beautiful Buddhist monastery in the country. Paro, located in the beautiful Paro Valley, is considered the gateway to Bhutan. It has the only airport in Bhutan.

An aerial view of Thimphu, the capital of Bhutan, one of the least populated capitals in the world.

HISTORY

Prayer flags at the Druk Wangyal Chorten. Throughout Bhutan, prayer flags of blue, green, red, yellow, and white are mounted on long poles and placed at both holy and dangerous sites. Bhutanese believe that the flags ward off demons and help to build merit.

BHUTAN'S HISTORY IS A MELTING pot that combines folklore, British explorers, Tibetan monks and soldiers, and rare manuscripts that have survived the feuds of warlords, earthquakes, and fires. Mystery cloaks Bhutan's distant past.

Bhutan's history is ambiguous, and for most of the Bhutanese, is incomprehensible without reference to at least some mythology, which the average Bhutanese regards as real as the actual history verified by ordinary material evidence.

A painting in traditional Bhutanese style of a Buddhist wheel of reincarnation in the grasp of the Monster of Impermanence. Buddhists believe that all life-forms experience an endless cycle of rebirths, and only through enlightenment can they be set free from this cycle.

From the time that historical records are clear, Bhutan has continuously and successfully defended its sovereignty. It is one of the only countries that has been independent throughout its entire history—never conquered, occupied, or governed by an outside power.

Nomadic yak herders moving their caravan toward the Lojula Pass in the Himalayan Mountains. Their lifestyle is not very much different from that of their ancestors' 4,000 years ago.

The strong belief in reincarnation means that important people may be known by several names. The times in which they lived are not always clearly distinguished. Similarly, the belief in Tantric Buddhism is so deeply embedded in Bhutanese life that a history of the country would make no sense without inclusion of the main religious teachers.

EARLY HISTORY

Bhutan has yet to undertake any real archaeological research. Thus any serious discovery could radically change the picture we have of the region's pre- and ancient history.

Man-made stone implements found on the surface and dating as early as 2000 B.C. suggest that the first inhabitants were nomadic herders who spent summers on the natural pasturage of the higher elevations, where it was unnecessary to cut down trees. In winter they lived in the more sheltered valleys, where firewood and forest foods were plentiful.

Little more than that is known about the first inhabitants. It is presumed that they practiced an animistic religion, which typically predated Buddhism in other parts of the Himalayas, but any further conjecture on their lifeways and beliefs must await the future findings of archaeologists.

BUDDHISM

The written history of Bhutan began with Buddhist literature and chronicles. Buddhism arrived in Bhutan in the seventh century when a Tibetan king, Srongtsen Gampo, ordered the construction of the first two Buddhist temples—one at Kyichu in the Paro Valley and the other at Jampel at Bumthang in central Bhutan. Both temples stand today and are popular with pilgrims.

In the eighth century, a Buddhist teacher known as Padmasambhava or Guru Rinpoche (Precious Master) brought the essence of Tantric Buddhism to Bhutan and Tibet, establishing the Nyingmapa school of thought. Bhutanese regard Guru Rinpoche as the Second Buddha because of the miraculous powers he was said to possess. The many sites at which Guru Rinpoche meditated are destinations of pilgrimage and devotion for most Bhutanese.

A golden image of Padmasambhava, or Guru Rinpoche in a nunnery near Tashigang. He is holding a *vajra* (a ritual weapon), a skull cup, and a trident with three severed heads.

The assassination of a Tibetan king in A.D. 842 cast Tibet into turmoil for two centuries. During this disordered time Tibetan aristocrats fled Tibet with their followers and settled in the central and eastern valleys of Bhutan. They took with them the seeds of the conflicts in Tibet, so until the 16th century, Bhutan suffered intermittent civil wars wherein almost every valley fought against its neighbors and in which none of the contending warlords could gain the upper hand.

Perched on a cliff overlooking the Paro Valley, the Taktsang Monastery is Bhutan's most photographed site. It is said that Guru Rinpoche flew here on the back of a tiger in the eighth century.

Against this tumultuous background, religious thought developed and segmented in Bhutan. Innovation arrived again from Tibet, this time by Phajo Drugom Shigpo in 1222. He waged a successful struggle against the Lhapas of western Bhutan and built monasteries at Phajoding and Tango. Phajo Drugom Shigpo taught the Bhutanese interpretations of the Drukpa (Drook-pah). *Druk* means thunder dragon, and *pa* refers to a sect and the people belonging to that particular Buddhist sect. Thus the name Drukpa came to Bhutan. Today the inhabitants who live in the western part of Bhutan, and by extension the citizens of the entire country, are known as Drukpa, which means "people of the thunder dragon."

UNIFICATION

China claimed Bhutan as a vassal state in the 19th century and mildly objected to British involvement.

For the first time in its history, Bhutan became politically unified in the 17th century under the lama Ngawang Namgyal, another religious leader from Tibet. Shabdrung Ngawang Namgyal (1594—1651) belonged to the Drukpa school and brought with him the title of Shabdrung, which translates as "at whose feet one prostrates." His authority in Tibet had been based on the determination that he was the reincarnation of a famous Drukpa scholar, Pema Karpo (1527—1592). After a series of victories over rival subsect leaders, Ngawang Namgyal became the first leader to unite Bhutan under one rule.

DRUKPA KUNLEY

One of the most popular figures in Bhutanese history was Drukpa Kunley (1455—1529), the patron saint of Bhutan. Known as "the divine madman" because of his shocking behavior, Drukpa Kunley was indeed an eccentric personality. An aristocrat from the great Gya family, he refused to take his monastic vows and instead wandered the country teaching Buddhism through songs. It is difficult to attribute historical significance to Drukpa Kunley, although every Bhutanese will place him among the most important historic national persons.

During his leadership Shabdrung Ngawang Namgyal introduced a dual system of government that distinguishes spiritual leaders from secular (government) leaders, called *desi*. He also introduced the system of *dzongs* in Bhutan, the first of which was constructed at Simtokha in the Wong River Valley. The *dzong* served as an impregnable fortress where the population could retreat in case of an attack. In addition, it housed a monastery and administrative offices. The same model of combined sectors of defense, religion, and administration was replicated in all subsequent *dzongs*.

Freed from the constant need for military defense, Shabdrung Ngawang Namgyal consolidated the political and religious powers of the Drukpas in western Bhutan. He turned his attention to diplomacy, winning rights to establish and control monasteries in Tibet and Nepal, where Bhutanese monasteries were to become among the most famous of Nepal's tourist sites at Boudanath and Swayanbunath, and where Bhutanese remained in charge until the Nepal-Tibet wars of 1854 to 1856. The Shabdrung did not live to see the full unification of central and eastern Bhutan, which was formally achieved in 1656, five years after his death in 1651.

With this unification Bhutan took on its definitive shape, but the country as a whole lacked a name. It was called variously Loh Jong (Southern Valleys), Loh Mon Kha Shi or Southern Mon (Country of Four Approaches), Loh Jong Men Jong (Southern Valleys of Medicinal Plants), and Loh Mon Tsenden Jong (Southern Mon Valleys Where Sandalwood and Cypress Grow). The Drukpas at last decided to name the country after themselves—Druk Yul, Land of the Thunder Dragon.

During his rule, Shabdrung Ngawang Namgyal gave Bhutan its system of administration and law. Buddhist moral principles and customary law of that time were fused into a national legal system, administered by a theocracy of monks headed by the je khenpo *(chief abbot) and a secular ruler or* desi. *The secular ruler presided over official and civil affairs, and the* je khenpo *ruled over the monastic community and religious affairs. The dual system of spiritual and temporal power was combined and supplanted by the person who became the Shabdrung, whose authority was at once that of the order of monks and the domain of secular law. The manner of the Shabdrung's leaving the tangible world was as remarkable as his reign, and in a sense he ruled from beyond the grave for over 50 years. In 1651 his closest aides announced that the Shabdrung had begun a strict retreat at Punakha Dzong. Lengthy retreats are common in Tantric Buddhism, where monks can spend years without any outside communication. Thus his failure to appear could be expected to attract little attention in a land where any news took weeks to travel from one end of the small country to the other.*

It is believed the Shabdrung actually died in 1651, although news of his death was concealed from the people by the desis *and* je khenpos *until 1705—an incredible period of 54 years, during which the people went on believing the Shabdrung was meditating on their behalf. Throughout this long interval Tibet attacked Bhutan repeatedly and was beaten back every time. Folklore claims that the Shabdrung gave the orders for the defense of Druk Yul.*

The Shabdrung system of power control called for a strong man at the top. Unfortunately, internal conflict emerged in the early 1700s, and power struggles among the dzongs *greatly watered down the Shabdrung's system of government. It was thus in a weakened state that Druk Yul was to encounter the power of the British.*

THE BRITISH

The British East India Company initially had little interest in Bhutan until the mountainous nation expanded into the kingdom of Cooch Behar on Bhutan's southern border in 1772. A request from the dethroned king of Cooch Behar for the intervention of the Honorable Company, as it called itself, resulted in a 1772 military action that expelled the Bhutanese and restored the king of Cooch Behar to his throne.

British officers and Indian troops drove the Bhutanese back into Bhutan and beat them in battles at Wong River, near Phuntsholing, and at Kalimpong, now in India on Bhutan's western flank. This British show of strength impressed the Bhutanese leadership. Failing to get help from Tibet, the new *desi*, or government leader, was eager to make an agreement with the British East India Company. In 1774 both parties signed a treaty in which the *desi* of Bhutan agreed to respect the territories of the East India Company and to permit the company to cut timber in Bhutan's forests.

Relations between the two countries remained friendly until 1826, when the British took control of Assam, which borders much of Bhutan's southern frontier. Very soon, control and occupation of the Duars area, which had been under Assamese control through a complex agreement with Bhutan, provoked conflict between the company and Bhutan's rulers.

Relations deteriorated until the British annexed the Bhutanese-controlled Assam Duars in 1841 in exchange for a compensation payment of 10,000 rupees a year to Bhutan. The East India Company's plans to clear the malarial forests and plant tea on Bhutan's slopes were shelved following British involvement in the Afghan War, the Anglo-Sikh War, and finally, the Indian Mutiny in 1857.

The Bhutanese took advantage of Britain's preoccupations to raid the company-controlled Duars and Cooch Behar, capturing elephants and kidnapping British subjects. The British were furious. Relations crashed downhill so badly that in November 1864 British forces marched into the remaining Duars area, seizing control of the whole of southern Bhutan. This Duar War (November 1864—April 1865) lasted only 5 months and, despite some battlefield victories by Bhutanese forces, ended in Bhutan's defeat and loss of part of its sovereign territory, and forced the cession of formerly occupied territories. This was not surprising considering that Bhutan had no regular army, and such forces that existed were composed of guards armed only with bows and arrows, swords, knives, and catapults, taking on the well-equipped British military. Bhutan had no choice but to sign away control of the Duars area in perpetuity to the British and to guarantee Britain's trade interests in return for an annual subsidy of 50,000 rupees. A year after Bhutan received the 50,000 rupees, the Duars strip was ceded to the East India Company.

With India's independence from Britain in 1947, Bhutan was recognized as an independent state. The two countries signed a treaty on August 9, 1949, in which most of the territory taken by Britain, including the Duars region, was returned (except for Kalimpong), and Bhutan agreed to be guided in its foreign affairs by India.

By that time the Shabdrung theocracy had been replaced by a formalized separation of religious and secular powers, with the secular realm under control of a hereditary monarchy, the Wangchuck dynasty, which rules Bhutan today. The title of Bhutan's head of state is Druk Gyalpo (Dragon King).

In the late 20th century several Assamese guerrilla groups seeking to establish an independent Assamese state in northeast India set up guerrilla bases in the forests of southern Bhutan from which they launched cross-border attacks on targets in Assam. The largest group was the ULFA (United Liberation Front of Assam). Negotiations aimed at removing them peacefully from these bases failed in the spring of 2003. The Bhutanese army successfully launched a large-scale operation in December 2003 to flush out these anti-India insurgents who were covertly operating training camps in southern Bhutan.

On December 17, 2005, the fourth king of Bhutan, Jigme Singye Wangchuck (born November 11, 1955), announced to a stunned nation that the first general elections would be held in 2008, and that he would abdicate the throne at that time in favor of his eldest son, the crown prince.

Jigme Khesar Namgyel Wangchuck was crowned on November 6, 2008. Bhutanese painted street signs, hung festive banners, and decorated traffic circles with fresh flowers to celebrate the occasion and welcome the new king. The young king, only 28 years old, began his unusual reign overseeing the democratization of his country by presiding over the last sessions of the still-seated parliament, where electoral laws, land reform, and other important domestic issues were being deliberated. He stated that the responsibility of this generation of Bhutanese is to ensure the success of democracy.

The youthful Bhutanese king has attracted a legion of female fans in Thailand, and the Thai press has dubbed him Prince Charming.

The world's youngest reigning monarch, King Jigme Khesar Namgyel Wangchuck smiles during his coronation at the ceremonial grounds of Tendrey Thang in Thimphu.

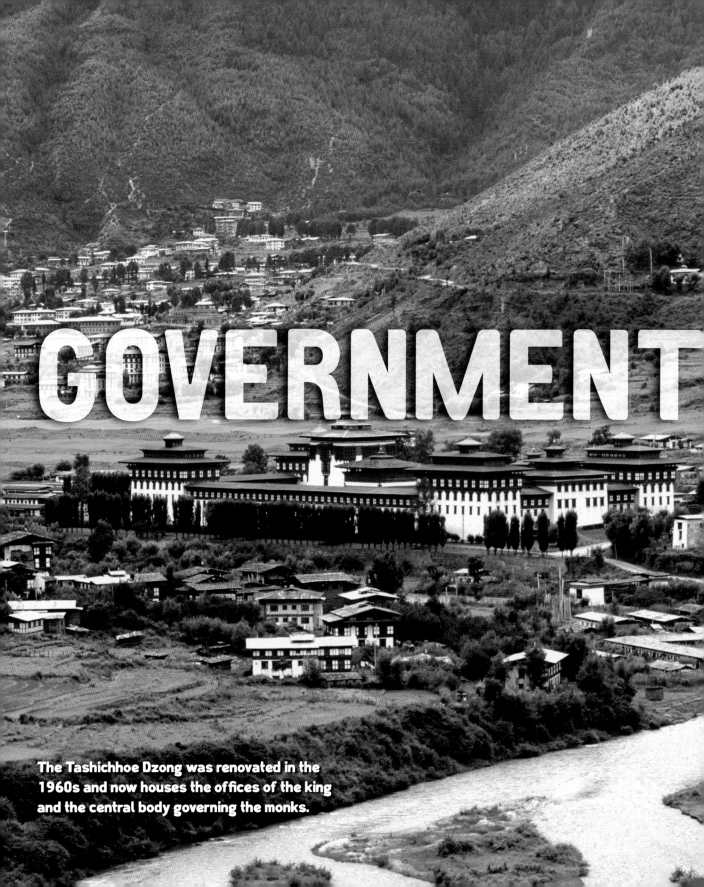

GOVERNMENT

The Tashichhoe Dzong was renovated in the 1960s and now houses the offices of the king and the central body governing the monks.

INTERNAL DISPUTES IN BHUTAN continued until 1885, when Ugyen Wangchuck defeated his political enemies and pulled Bhutan under one rule, ending several civil wars and rebellions from 1882 to 1885. At that time, British power was dominant all across the Indian subcontinent, and Ugyen Wangchuck favored increased cooperation with the British.

In 1904 Ugyen accompanied the British invasion of Tibet and assisted in a negotiated settlement between Tibet and Britain. In recognition of his services and status, he was awarded the British title of Knight Commander of the Indian Empire.

A stately military parade in Thimphu.

The government of Bhutan had been a traditional absolute monarchy, but has now evolved into a constitutional monarchy. The peaceful march to democracy has been a steady one. Although the king's role is hereditary, he can be removed by a two-thirds majority vote by the parliament.

Villagers discussing issues in the local community, preparing for a meeting with government officials. King Jigme Dorji Wangchuck took the initiative to adapt Bhutan's system of government to the modern era.

Following three decades of peace under the rule of Ugyen, the secular and religious leaders came together and unanimously elected him king of Bhutan. On December 17, 1907, Ugyen Wangchuck was crowned with the title Druk Gyalpo (Dragon King), and Bhutan's present system of hereditary monarchy began with the Wangchuck dynasty.

GLORIOUS ISOLATION

Good relations with its neighbors on the subcontinent and with Britain did not change Bhutan's policy of isolation. The second king of Bhutan, Jigme Wangchuck, succeeded his father, Ugyen Wangchuck, and ruled from 1926 to 1952, a tumultuous time that saw the Great Depression, World War II, and violent independence movements in many corners of the world.

The outside world had little to offer Bhutan, and Bhutan, having never been colonized, had little need to open its doors. King Jigme therefore concentrated his efforts on strengthening the internal administrative and taxation systems, as well as centralizing control over a country that remained geographically fractured into valleys and *dzongs*. Bhutan's ongoing isolationism endowed the small state with decades of peace at home, in contrast to the conflicts beyond its borders.

This isolation was not absolute, however. King Jigme Wangchuck sent his son and heir to India and England to be educated. Financial aid from Britain enabled the construction of the first Western-style schools in Bhutan and was also used to send the first Bhutanese students to India for advanced education. English began to be taught in the schools.

MODERNIZATION

When the third king, Jigme Dorji Wangchuck, succeeded his father in 1952, he wasted no time in gently leading Bhutan toward modernization. He was the prime mover in Bhutan's slow transition from an absolute monarchy to a constitutional monarchy. He abolished slavery and serfdom in 1956 and invited the Indian prime minister, Jawaharlal Nehru, for an official visit in 1958. With China wresting control of Tibet on Bhutan's northern border, it became obvious to the king that isolationism was no longer the best survival tactic.

The progressive monarch launched Bhutan's first five-year plan in 1961 with an emphasis on road building and the construction of the huge Chhukha River hydroelectric project. In 1962 Bhutan joined the Colombo Plan, an international organization that promotes cooperation in economics and social development in Asia and the Pacific, thus gaining access to technical assistance and training facilities. In 1966 the king moved the capital to Thimphu to increase the efficiency of government administration. Bhutan joined the United Nations in 1971. It also established formal diplomatic relations with another nation for the first time, by allowing an Indian ambassador to reside in Bhutan and sending an ambassador to India to represent Bhutan.

King Jigme Dorji's achievements were impressive. Dzongkha (dzong-kha) was proclaimed the national language of Bhutan in 1961. He also set up Bhutan's Tshogdu (National Assembly) in 1953 and drew up a 12-volume written code of law. He redistributed land to the poor, imposed equal land revenue, created the Royal Bhutan Army, and introduced a national police force. In 1968 he separated the judiciary from the executive by establishing the Thrimkong Gongma, the High Court. He carried out other development projects, including the establishment of a national museum in Paro, a national library, and national archives, and built a national stadium. Because of his progressive initiatives, he is regarded as the Father of Modern Bhutan. The present monarch, Jigme Khesar Namgyel Wangchuck (the fifth king of Bhutan), has overseen the nation's first elections, and has also traveled extensively around the country, speaking mainly to the youth of Bhutan on the need for Bhutanese to strive for greater standards, stressing the need for people of a small country to work smarter than those of stronger ones.

On August 8, 1949, Bhutan and India signed a treaty whereby India agreed not to interfere in Bhutan's internal relations, while Bhutan agreed "to be guided by the advice of the Government of India in regard to its external relations." In February 2007 the treaty was revised, deleting references to all such phrases as "will be guided," thus eliminating any lingering doubts about the sovereign and independent status of Bhutan.

King Jigme Dorji Wangchuck, the third king, died in 1972 at the young age of 44. His son, Jigme Singye Wangchuck, ascended the throne on June 2, 1974, at the age of 19.

Bhutan's lifelong era of isolation ended upon his coronation, an occasion witnessed for the first time by the international press. The young king was credited as being the architect of modern education, the creator of Bhutan's free national health service, a builder of roads, an initiator of conservation programs, a reformer, and a diplomat. Under his leadership, Bhutan joined most UN agencies, the Movement of Non-Aligned Countries, and the South Asian Association for Regional Cooperation. He broadened diplomatic representation to 21 countries, including Bangladesh, India, Japan, Switzerland, and the European Community, a forerunner of the European Union. Gradually, he lifted restrictions on foreigners visiting Bhutan. In an effort to modernize Bhutan's political system and reduce the magisterial power of the monarch, King Jigme Singye Wangchuck introduced a package of democratic reforms that granted power to the legislature, through a legal vote of no confidence, to depose the king in favor of his successor—preserving, nevertheless, the monarchy.

While notable progress in political, economic, and social spheres had been accomplished in a short period, the king had been considerate of the need to conserve the environment and retain the unique character of Bhutan's people, while promoting national identity built on traditional values. He listed his developmental goals as national self-reliance; sustainability; efficiency and enhancement of the private sector; people's participation and decentralization; human resource enrichment; and last, regionally balanced change. While economic self-reliance is Bhutan's goal, commercial interests must be in harmony with the policy of environmental conservation and must work for the greater benefit of "One Nation, One People," the Bhutanese motto. The king himself summed up his policy goals in the felicitous phrase "gross national happiness."

THE CENTRAL GOVERNMENT

In 1999 Jigme Singye Wangchuck, the fourth king, created a body called the Lhengye Zhungtshog (Council of Ministers). The king is the head of state—assisted by a cabinet consisting of ministers and representatives from the full range of ministries and special commissions—and the chief of the army and police. Executive power is exercised by the Lhengye Zhungtshog, with legislative power vested both in the government and the former Grand National Assembly. Every ministry is divided into departments, each headed by a director.

NATIONAL ASSEMBLY

The National Assembly is the elected lower house of Bhutan's new bicameral parliament that also consists of the Druk Gyalpo (the king) and the National Council. The National Assembly today has 47 members, who were elected in the first-ever general elections on March 24, 2008. The National Council, consisting of 25 members, is the upper house of Bhutan's parliament. The king appoints 5 members of the National Council, and the remaining 20 are elected by the electorates of the 20 districts, the equivalent of states, of Bhutan. The members cannot belong to any political party and must have the minimum qualification of graduation from a recognized university.

Bhutanese citizens registering with officials to cast their votes in the general elections at a polling place.

The members of the first National Council are generally young, aged below 40. This is attributed to the law that only persons holding a college degree are eligible to be candidates and that access to formal education is relatively recent in Bhutan.

ECONOMY

Farmers on their way home after
a long day of harvesting the
fertile fields of the Paro Valley.

CHAPTER 4

The Bhutanese monetary system is based on the ngultrum, which was established in 1974.

DEVELOPMENT PROJECTS AND THE modernization of health services, education, telecommunications, postal service, roads, and public transportation have greatly increased Bhutanese interaction with the outside world in recent decades.

Despite visible developments, the daily life of most Bhutanese has changed very little since the 17th century. About 80 percent of the population is dependent on farming, at least to feed their own families. They use the same tools as their forefathers, grow the same subsistence crops, use oxen to pull their plows, and come together in kinship and

A small grocery store in Thimphu caters to the daily needs of the local population.

The National Post Office and bank along Chang lam in Thimphu is an institute where the famous Bhutanese stamps are displayed and sold.

neighborhood groups to share labor-intensive activities. Such farmers might listen to a radio and hear the news from India, but they are more likely to aspire to own a horse than an automobile. Apart from public services and small-scale private enterprises, employment in the modern sectors of the economy remains limited.

SOURCES OF REVENUE

Agriculture and forestry are rightly regarded as the main pillars of Bhutan's economy, because the great majority of its people could not survive without them. These sectors provide the primary livelihood for more than 90 percent of the population. With the opening up of Bhutan, in 2010, export revenues jumped by nearly 50 percent from the previous year.

AGRICULTURE AND LIVESTOCK

Above the subtropical line, where access to a cash market is problematic, priority is placed on growing subsistence food grains to feed the farming family. All farmers keep livestock to produce milk products and provide draft power. At higher altitudes, little cultivation is possible, but there are wide areas of natural grasslands that provide pasture for cattle, sheep, and yaks.

Official emphasis on self-sufficiency has ensured that most Bhutanese maintain their own family plots where they can grow enough to feed the family. Anyone who feels he does not have enough land can petition the king for more; such petitions are frequently granted.

Given that a significant percentage of agricultural land has been destroyed to make way for infrastructure in the country, and the migration from villages into towns has resulted in a shortage of labor in the countryside, Bhutan has gradually shifted from being a net exporter to a net importer of rice. Bhutan now imports 6,614 to 7,716 tons (6,000 to 7,000 metric tons) of rice every year. There has been a reduction in the area of cultivation, food production has become restricted to subsistence, and the livestock population has decreased. Other alarming developments such as increases in the cost of farming, low crop yields, and insufficient food are also observed with increasing frequency. Farmers themselves have suggested two ways to alleviate the problem. The first is improving rural areas by raising the standard of living and the quality of life to discourage rural-urban migration. The second is making farming more profitable by introducing efficient agricultural technologies and revamping the marketing and distribution system in the country.

Only 7.7 percent of the land is under cultivation, and most of that is in the wealthier south.

A farmer carrying a full basket across a buckwheat field in the Phobjikha Valley.

The Punak Chhu River in Wangdü Phodrang. Bhutan's fast-flowing rivers provide abundant potential hydroelectricity, helping to support capital-intensive industries such as forestry and mining.

HYDROELECTRICITY

It is estimated that Bhutan has the potential to generate 30,000 megawatts (MW) of hydroelectric power. Currently, the Chhukha project generates but a tiny fraction of that potential, producing 336 MW, of which 78 percent is exported. The Tala Dam, on the Wong River, was opened with much fanfare in May 2008 by ministers from both Bhutan and India. Bhutan's current hydropower capacity is 1,480 MW, and it plans additional projects to generate 10,000 MW of new power by 2020, almost entirely for export to India, whose energy needs are ravenous. Work has also begun on a 19-mile (30-km) rail link between the border towns of Hashimara in West Bengal and Phuntsholing in Bhutan. Bangladesh is hoping to hop on the bandwagon and purchase electricity from Bhutan as well. There are smaller projects of 60 MW near Mongar and Wangdü Phodrang. Given Bhutan's source potential and the energy needs of an industrializing India, the government's plan to fund Bhutan's entire national budget from revenues obtained from the sale of hydroelectricity appears realistic and within reach.

Bhutan's hydroelectric projects are consistent with the national philosophy of development, as they harness the awesome power of Bhutan's rivers without building large dams. As such, the hydroelectric projects do not require the sacrifice of large areas of productive farmland, are clean, and may be regarded as environmentally friendly.

One development project rejected by Bhutan was the expansion of its domestic silk industry. This would have required dropping silkworm cocoons alive into boiling water to ensure long threads of silk. Instead, Bhutanese wait for the silkworms to eat their way out of their silk cocoons, thus allowing the living creatures to fulfill their destiny. This natural process yields shorter lengths of silk threads that result in a slightly coarser cloth.

POWER TO THE PEOPLE

Hydroelectric projects exist in areas where they can produce the greatest benefit for the smallest outlay of funds and labor, and where they are near to the buyer. To construct transmission lines to serve all of Bhutan's scattered population, however, would be unsightly and expensive. About 96 percent of urban households enjoy the benefits of electricity, whereas only 40 percent of rural households are electrified. This contributes to the high rates of deforestation, as many rural households depend on fuelwood for their energy needs. According to the Department of Energy (DOE), Bhutan consumed 798,716 tons (724,595 metric tons) of firewood in 2005, which accounted for 59 percent of the total primary energy supply. The Bhutanese government is trying to strike a balance between bringing the marvels of electricity to all of Bhutan while preserving the beautiful environment at the same time.

Through its electricity purchases from Bhutan, the government of India funds nearly 60 percent of Bhutan's budget expenditures.

Power cables in Bhutan. Rural locals now get to experience the benefits of electricity, too.

FORESTRY

Before hydroelectric power and other modern energy sources were available, wood was the nearly exclusive source of fuel for heating, cooking, and lighting. The provision of electricity, as well as better regulation of fuelwood collection and more aggressive reforestation projects, is a key factor in forest conservation. Because affordable electricity is not available throughout the land, the government has established fuelwood plantations near villages to accommodate daily needs and to promote forest conservation.

Recognizing the potential value of its forestry resource, Bhutan became increasingly conscientious about forestry management in the 1970s. In 1977, the World Wildlife Fund began supporting Bhutan's forest management through organizing forest ranger training programs, supplying funds for forest boundary demarcation, building guard posts, and constructing a patrol road for what later would be named the Royal Manas National Park. Bhutan rejected the World Bank's aid to build a major dam on the Manas Chhu River in 1986 that would have flooded this major conservation area on the southern Bhutan-India border.

Logs being transported to sawmills from a forest, taxing the truck's load capacity.

By 1989 Bhutan had developed nine other forest and wildlife preserves, also mostly along their southern frontier with India. In the face of increasing denuded hillsides, private logging was banned, and strict standards for public-sector logging operations were established in 1979. Farmers were warned against burning off forests to clear land for cultivation—the ancient slash-and-burn practice—and forest guards were trained in increasing numbers to help preserve the valuable resources. Wildlife sanctuaries also were developed. One of the immediate results of forestry sector regulation, however, was a sharp drop in revenue from forestry since the late 1970s. With assistance from the United Nations Development Programme (UNDP) and the World Wildlife Fund, the government established a trust fund for environmental conservation in 1991.

Workers at a sawmill in Bhutan. Forest products are near the top of Bhutan's natural resources. The nation carefully balances revenue and ecology in this significant industry.

EXPORT INDUSTRIES

Bhutan is one of the least industrialized countries in the world and is not lamenting that label. There is no indication that an industrial revolution will ever arrive in Bhutan, and even if it did, it would certainly be resisted by the government. This is not to say that Bhutanese have turned their backs on the benefits of modernization. They simply prefer to keep what they have before trying anything new. Moreover, anything new must conform to the values of society, be environmentally friendly, and use resources prudently. On a global scale, that would be a tall order.

Apples being wrapped for shipment throughout the country and abroad.

Bhutan seems destined to succeed because it has a small population contrasted with its resources, as well as an abundance of potential clean and sustainable energy. The majority of its population, who are Buddhists, also express a positive attitude. They see conservation and sustainability as intrinsically good. The priority is always to maintain subsistence production and feed the family; therefore, production exceeding basic needs must not take people away from their land at significant times. Given this background, it is perhaps surprising that Bhutan has managed to build an export industry around an apparently all-gain-and-no-pain process.

Good quality furniture is an example of Bhutan's export production, in this case destined for India. Matsutake mushrooms are cultivated in the west of the country and exported to Japan, Singapore, and Thailand. Bhutan's temperate fruits find markets in neighboring countries and serve as the base for a growing industry of canning fruit and making jams, which, along with various types of alcoholic beverages, are marketed cheaply under the Druk label to India, Nepal, and more distant buyers. Oranges are a major export. A cement factory sends large quantities of cement to India and Bangladesh.

One successful new enterprise fully in line with the national philosophy is the production of oil from lemongrass. The villagers use comparatively simple equipment to distill the oil from the fast-growing weed, which should be cut down anyway. The product is small and easily transportable, making it an ideal enterprise for the remote eastern villages where the industry has grown up. About 29 tons (26 metric tons) of lemongrass oil is produced annually. Bhutan sells its best-quality material to Europe and lower grades to India, where it goes into perfumes and deodorants. The profits return directly to villagers, who use the money to improve their farming methods and purchase some of the conveniences of the modern world. So successful has the project been that the villages are now diversifying into pine oil and the oils of other plants that thrive in Bhutan, such as rhododendron and juniper.

Burt Todd (1924—2006), a businessman and adventurer who may have been the first American to visit the kingdom of Bhutan, assisted in establishing a postage stamp program in Bhutan in 1962. Bhutan has become known for the unusual designs of its postage stamps, which were originally chosen by Todd specifically to attract publicity. The Bhutan stamp program was set up to raise money for the improvement of Bhutan's infrastructure after the country was denied a loan from the World Bank. Many Bhutanese stamps depict the nation's *dzong* architecture, Buddhist heritage, wildlife, and sport. The sport stamps celebrate the Olympics and soccer World Cups. Coinlike stamps were issued in 1966, 1968, and 1975. Moreover, 3-D stamp series were also produced, with the first issues released in 1967 depicting astronauts and lunar modules. Unique molded plastic 3-D stamps of ancient artifacts were released in 1971 and of famous people in 1972. In 2008 the *Bhutan Post* issued the first CD-Rom postage stamps in the world.

Beehives producing honey in a mountain village. Cottage industries, wherein residents make and sell small produce at home, are common in rural settlements.

TOURISM

The 1974 coronation of the fourth king, His Majesty Jigme Singye Wangchuck, was witnessed by the international media and many foreigners, marking Bhutan's stepping out onto the world stage. Previously, any foreign visitors to Bhutan had come as guests of the king or other members of the royal family. The visitors who attended the ceremony were welcomed as guests, and housing was specially built for them. When they left, these lodgings were made available to the first small groups of tourists.

The Zangdhopelri Hotel in Punakha welcomes upscale visitors from afar.

Bhutan is prone to natural disasters, especially during monsoon seasons, and access roads to remote areas may be closed for up to half a year.

Tourism in Bhutan began in 1974, the coronation year, when the government of Bhutan, in an effort to raise revenue and to promote the country's unique culture and traditions to the outside world, opened its cloistered country to foreigners. Despite now being open, the government was acutely aware of the environmental impact tourists could have on Bhutan's unique and virtually unspoiled landscape and culture. Therefore, it restricted the level of tourist activity from the start, preferring higher quality tourism. Entry is free for citizens of India and Bangladesh. All other tourists, however, must travel on a preplanned package that costs a hefty $200 fee for every day they stay in Bhutan. Independent travel is not permitted in Bhutan. Nonetheless, in 2009, 23,480 tourists entered the country. As in all of its ventures with the outside world, Bhutan embarked on tourism with pervasive caution. The Bhutanese are determined to preserve their unique culture, and thus when in doubt, they stop, set rules and regulations, and monitor cautiously before making any relaxations in their protective codes. This development philosophy has kept the character of the country largely intact and made Bhutan an even more attractive tourist experience.

TRANSPORTATION

Before the 1960s, transportation—even for royalty visiting abroad—meant travel by foot and mule back, many days between destinations, and with primitive facilities all the way. The first roads that were built in the early 1960s followed the old north-south routes of Bhutan's Duars, connecting Thimphu and other towns in the central axis of the country with the Indian border to the south. By this means, centers of population and administration were physically connected to India, each in its own line, but not to each other.

The country's primary road now is the East-West highway, known locally as the Lateral Road. Its construction was started in 1962. The road begins in Phuntsholing on the southwest Indian border and terminates in Tashigang in the far east, with spurs to other main centers such as Paro, Thimphu, and Punakha. The Lateral Road is built to a standard width of only 8.2 feet (2.5 m) yet must support traffic in both directions. The cost of cutting a wider road through the mountainous Middle Himalayas is prohibitive at this time. Safety barriers, road markings, and signage are sparse. Traffic moves at a slow speed, typically around 9 miles per hour (15 km/h), to minimize head-on collisions. Road accidents still occur frequently and, because of the steep

The narrow highway over the Dochu La Pass, leading from Thimphu to Punakha. Prior to the construction of roads in the 1960s, travel in Bhutan was either by foot or on mule back or horseback.

In Bhutan buses are operated by government-owned as well as private companies.

The Paro International Airport. Druk Air, Bhutan's national airline, operates between Paro and India, Nepal, Bangladesh, and Thailand.

mountainous topography, are typically horrific. Most of the route between Paro Airport and Thimphu, nevertheless, has recently been improved to a two-lane road. Because much of the geologic formation is unstable, there are frequent slips and landslides, which are aggravated by summer monsoons, winter snowstorms, and frost heave conditions. Teams of Indian laborers are housed and fed at work camps in the mountain passes to be dispatched to clear the routes in the event of road blockage. Conditions in the work camps are wretched, with the workers reduced to breaking rock into gravel on a piece-rate basis when they are not clearing the roads. An international aid project is under way, however, to stabilize the worst sections of the road. A major Japanese endeavor seeks to replace most of the narrow one-way bridges with two-way beam spans capable of carrying heavier traffic. Most freight is moved on 8-ton (7.26-metric ton) trucks, which are often overloaded. There is a network of passenger buses also. The most common vehicle in governmental and private use alike is the four-wheel drive pickup truck. A national driver licensing system includes a driving test, but this is not rigorous. Government drivers are trained at the Samthang Vocational Training Institute driving school (formerly the National Driving Training Institute), or they can learn on the job as "handy boys."

The single runway at Paro Airport is located in a steep-sided valley with restricted Visual Flight Rules (VFR) approaches. During a monsoon season, flights are often delayed by cloud cover. Drukair is the national carrier, connecting Paro to Bangkok (Thailand); Dhaka (Bangladesh); Kolkata, Gaya,

Bagdogra, and Delhi (India); and Kathmandu (Nepal). Drukair replaced its two aging Bae-146 four-engine jets in 2004 with faster and more capacious Airbus A319-100 aircraft.

DEVELOPMENT AID AND PHILOSOPHY

In December 2004 Bhutan became the first country in the world to ban smoking and the selling of tobacco.

The Bhutanese way of life can be summed up by the prevailing philosophy of gross national happiness. Druk Gyalpo Jigme Singye Wangchuck decided to define the nation's priority not as its gross domestic product (GDP) but its GNH. The king suggested that the progress of nations be measured by gross national happiness—for the rich are not always happy while the happy generally consider themselves rich. While conventional development models stress economic growth as the ultimate objective, the concept of GNH claims to be based on the premise that true development of human society can happen when material and spiritual well-being occur side by side to complement and reinforce each other.

GNH consists of four pillars that embody national and local values, aesthetics, and spiritual traditions:

1. Equitable and equal socioeconomic development;
2. Preservation and promotion of cultural and spiritual heritage;
3. Conservation of environment; and
4. Good governance, which is interwoven, complementary, and consistent with the other three pillars.

The Happy Planet Index estimates that the average level of life satisfaction in Bhutan lies within the top 10 percent of nations worldwide and certainly is higher than other nations with similar levels of GDP per capita.

Bhutan is genuinely grateful for the substantial international aid it gets, but places a greater value on the conservation of the Bhutanese way of life, Bhutanese social principles, and the environment of Bhutan.

By 2015 or sooner, Bhutan plans to be self-reliant, so that foreign aid will no longer be needed to sustain its development program. Much of this happy outcome will depend on the sale of hydroelectricity. If things go according to plan, the sale of energy to India will more than cover the entire national budget, enabling Bhutan to maintain its own pace of development.

ENVIRONMENT

The Drukgyel Village in Bhutan. Bhutan's fertile valleys are teeming with loosely organized villages that dot the terraced farmlands against the lush forests.

CHAPTER 5

FOR CENTURIES THE BHUTANESE have treasured their natural environment and have looked upon it reverently as the source of all life. This traditional devotion to nature has delivered Bhutan into the 21st century with an environment still richly intact. The country wishes to continue living in harmony with nature and to pass on this precious heritage to its future generations.

Nowhere in the Himalayas is the natural heritage more rich and varied than in Bhutan. In historical records the kingdom was called the Valley of Medicinal Herbs, a name that applies to this day.

A signpost in Gangtey urges the public not to litter.

Fortunately for Bhutan, maintaining a balanced natural ecosystem remains the central theme of its development initiatives. The country refuses to sacrifice its natural resource base for short-term economic gains. Its plans are consistent with the central tenets of sustainable development, environmental conservation, and cultural values. Bhutan was named in 1998 as one of the top 10 biodiversity hot spots in the world because of its remarkably high concentration of plant and animal species in its forests. It has been identified as one of the 221 global endemic bird area centers.

The country signed the Convention on Biological Diversity and United Nations Framework Convention on Climate Change in Rio de Janeiro in 1992. These conventions were ratified in 1995 at the 73rd session of the National Assembly. The Royal Government of Bhutan has also made a national commitment to uphold its obligation to future generations by charting a plan of progress called the Middle Path—this is a way that upholds both environmental and cultural preservation as integral parts of the development process.

AIR POLLUTION

Unlike its neighboring countries in the South Asia region and with the rest of Asia, air pollution is not yet an acute problem in Bhutan, but it is an emerging concern. Despite cautious oversight, Bhutan is undergoing rapid industrialization and urbanization. The industrial sector in Bhutan grew by about 200 percent over a 5-year period (1997—2002). About 33 percent of the population now lives in cities compared with some 5 percent only 10 years ago. Bhutan's urban population as a whole is increasing at 6.7 percent annually. It is estimated that by the year 2020, half the population of Bhutan will live in cities. In urban areas the number of vehicles and industries have been increasing speedily, and sadly, incidences of urban air pollution are becoming more conspicuous.

In Thimphu the primary causes of deteriorating air quality are vehicle emissions and heating appliances using fuelwood. Apart from its being an aesthetic intrusion in the capital city, the poor air has increased the frequency of respiratory diseases. The government of Bhutan banned

the importing of reconditioned cars from third-world countries in 2000, as such cars were heavy emitters of pollutants such as carbon monoxide. The vehicle count in Bhutan grew by 14 percent in 2007 alone, pushing up the number from 14,206 to 16,335.

The problem of emissions is aggravated by the inferior quality of fuel available in Bhutan. Diesel fuel has high sulfur (0.25 percent) and wax contents, and diesel-using vehicles are not fitted with high-altitude compensators. As a result, those vehicles emit a lot of soot. Diesel vehicles are three times more polluting than gasoline ones. The lower price of diesel fuel leads to a larger number of diesel vehicles on the roads. Diesel engine vehicles are also kept idling for a longer period—a minimum of 15 minutes to warm up an engine during the winter, resulting in higher levels of pollutants being pumped into the environment. As of July 2010, higher-grade fuel has been introduced in Bhutan, which is expected to curb pollution somewhat by reducing the emission of carbon monoxide and other harmful pollutants.

It is believed that fuelwood is the primary source of energy for about 65,000 households in rural areas. This is the second major contributor to air pollution. In rural Bhutan an open fire inside the house is commonly used for cooking, heating, and lighting. There are neither chimneys nor proper ventilation systems. Owing to inefficient combustion, large amounts of incompletely burned materials are rendered to smoke and irritating gases. The use of more efficient stoves and processed forms of biomass (charcoal, biogas, or methanol), together with the adoption of simple ventilation measures, help to reduce indoor air pollution and to mitigate the health risks associated with the combustion of biomass fuels. It has been recommended

Improved roadways have invited the rapid increase of the number of vehicles in Bhutan, dumping exhaust pollutants onto the once pristine corner of the earth. Viewed here is a busy gas station in Thimphu.

that the government ban the use of woodstoves in cities and promote energy-efficient electrical appliances for heating and cooking purposes. More emphasis needs to be placed on supplying electrical connections in rural areas to gradually replace woodstoves. The faster Bhutan's abundant electricity is brought to every threshold in the country, the surer the forests of this beautiful Shangri-la will be preserved.

DEFORESTATION

Deforestation is taking place mainly due to infrastructure development, expansion of industrial and agricultural activities, and increasing urbanization. The strong conservation ethic of the Bhutanese people, however, and the political will of its government are the greatest contributing factors in the preservation of the forests. The National Assembly has mandated the country to maintain a minimum of 60 percent of the land area under forest cover for all time. Different acts and programs have been ordered by the Royal Government of Bhutan to minimize the rate of deforestation.

A woman carrying firewood for fuel at a rural village in Bhutan. Poor combustion in home fires creates toxic air pollutants.

WASTE DISPOSAL

Waste disposal is an emerging problem in almost every growing town in Bhutan. The increase in waste generation can be attributed primarily to factors such as rapid rates of urbanization, rural-urban migration, changing consumption patterns, and a high population growth rate. While the size of the problem is relatively small and manageable in rural communities, it appears to be growing significantly in urban areas. With the Solid Waste Management Act of December 2007, environment inspectors can fine those who are caught littering or illegally dumping solid waste in and around

PASAKHA—THE POLLUTION CAPITAL OF BHUTAN

Pasakha, about 9 miles (14 km) from Phuntsholing, is poised to become Bhutan's first major industrial town. It is already home to several large industries—Bhutan Carbide and Chemicals Limited (BCCL), Bhutan Ferro Alloys Limited (BFAL), and Tashi Carbon, all of which were established in the early 1990s. Other factories include the expanded and upgraded Druk cement plant and a furniture unit of the Bhutan Board Products Limited (BBPL). More recently, Bhutan Beverages Company Limited (BBCL), a soft drink bottling plant under the Tashi Group, began commercial production in Pasakha in 2010. There are also several other small- and medium-sized industries that have been established in Pasakha in the last few years. Pasakha is ideal for mineral-based industries because mineral sources are close by. Quartz, dolomite, and limestone are available in Pachina, Kamji, Tintali, and Gomtu, less than 62 miles (100 km) away. Pasakha's proximity to the Indian border enables easy movement and marketing of products and the importation of raw materials, labor, and transportation.

Unfortunately, upward-spiraling Pasakha is also becoming the pollution capital of Bhutan. Smoke billowing from the chimneys of industries in Pasakha has caught the attention of travelers along the Thimphu-Phuntsholing highway, which is now routed along the Pasakha-Manitar road. Children in Pasakha living near industrial pollution sources or areas of heavy traffic, and lacking adequate medical attention, nourishment, or sanitary living conditions, are at greatest danger from the toxic effects of air pollution on their respiratory systems and are also at risk of developing allergies, asthma, or cancer.

the capital, Thimphu. The new act is based on the concept of 3 R's—reduce, recycle, and reuse.

Since 2002, the waste generated daily in Thimphu has alarmingly more than tripled from 12 to 39 tons (11—35 metric tons). In Thimphu the solid waste is disposed of at the sanitary landfill site at Meymeylhakha, which is the only landfill site in all of Bhutan. The site is now being enlarged to accommodate more waste. The total waste being treated at the landfill is currently at 8 to 10 tons (7—9 metric tons) a day. Unless the Bhutanese government takes serious steps to address the issue, the waste problem will become an unmanageable monolith in the very near future.

RECYCLING

Currently about 20 percent of collected waste in Bhutan is sent for recycling. Valuable waste products, mostly metal scrap, beer bottles, and cans, are exported to India and Bangladesh because of insufficient recycling facilities at home. Certain quantities of waste plastics and paper, mainly cardboards, are also exported, but not as much or as often as the metals and the bottles. Organic waste is never composted and no formal waste sorting systems exist. Only 40 to 50 percent of Thimphu's waste is hauled to the Meymeylhakha disposal site directly. The rest is either dumped into municipal drains or rivers, clogging and flooding them, or partially burned in open pits by individual householders. The municipalities also are failing to enforce the law against littering. Nevertheless, there are some success stories of waste recycling ventures in Thimphu. Among them are the sawdust briquetting venture at Ramtokto (Thimphu), metal scrap recycling, and PET (polyethylene terephthalate) bottle recycling.

SAWDUST RECYCLING Until early 2005 sawdust generated by the sawmills had been a concern across the country, especially in Thimphu. Water pollution and sawdust irritation to the surrounding inhabitants during the windy season impelled the government to search for alternative solutions. The high rate of firewood consumption was also depleting forest resources around Thimphu. The Forestry Development Corporation Limited (FDCL) established a sawdust briquetting plant at Ramtokto in the outskirts of Thimphu that compacted the sawdust into blocks. This plant substantially disposed of the sawdust generated in Thimphu and Paro by substituting sawdust briquettes for firewood, reducing pressure on the local forest resources and setting up a win-win solution for all concerned.

METAL AND ELECTRONIC WASTE RECYCLING Tin scrap and electronic waste hardware are exported in bulk to India by scrap dealers and waste pickers—people who sort mixed waste and sell it to the recycling companies. Aluminum and copper waste items are consumed locally by traditional Bhutanese metal fabricating units and others across the Indian border.

The Karma scrap dealer in Thimphu alone annually exports an average 5 tons (4.5 metric tons) of metal scrap to India and Bangladesh.

BOTTLE RECYCLING Bottles made of PET are recycled to reuse the plastic out of which they are made and to reduce the amount of waste going into landfills. In collaboration with the hotel and restaurant owners of Paro, and with the support of the National Environment Commission (NEC), the Paro Dzongkhag Administration has set up a PET bottle-crushing unit in Paro. In Thimphu, the Bhutan Beverages Limited Company has established a similar unit with support from the Thimphu City Corporation. The Bhutan Agro Industry in Serbithang, Thimphu, which bottles spring water, has also obtained a PET bottle-crushing machine to assist in PET bottle waste management.

PAPER RECYCLING The wastepaper recycling unit of the Jungshi Handmade Paper Factory in Thimphu processes all sorts of wastepapers, including cardboard boxes. The recycled products are paper sheets that can be reused as packing materials and containers, envelopes, and toys. When the recycling unit is fully utilized, it will consume 5 to 6 tons (4.5 to 5 metric tons) of discarded paper daily.

A papermaker at work at the Jungshi Handmade Paper Factory in Thimphu.

The majestic snow leopard, at home in isolated Bhutan, is critically endangered.

CONSERVATION

Bhutan is seen as a model for proactive conservation initiatives. The kingdom has received international acclaim for its staunch commitment to the maintenance of its biodiversity. This is reflected in its decision to maintain at least 60 percent of the land area under forest cover; to designate more than a quarter of its territory as national parks, reserves, and other protected areas; and most recently, to identify a further 9 percent of land area as biodiversity corridors linking the protected areas. Environmental conservation has been placed at the core of the nation's development strategy. It is not treated as a sector but rather as a whole set of concerns that must be mainstreamed in Bhutan's overall approach to development planning and to be buttressed by the force of law.

WILDLIFE

Along its southern border, the narrow tropical and subtropical belt supports the Asiatic elephant, greater one-horned rhinoceros, gaur (a large wild ox), wild water buffalo, hog deer, tiger, clouded leopard, and other mammals. Only 93 miles (150 km) to the north, high Himalayan fauna include the blue sheep, takin, musk deer, snow leopard, and wolf. So far 770 species of birds have been recorded in Bhutan, including the hornbill. Moreover, the country is famous for its wintering population (about 260 birds) of the vulnerable black-necked crane in the valleys of Phobjikha, Bumdeling, and Gyetsa.

DHOLE The dhole is a wild dog, a wolflike animal weighing 27 to 44 pounds (12—20 kg), native to Southeast Asia. Dholes are highly social animals, living in large clans of around 25 members, which occasionally split up into smaller packs to hunt. Though fearful of humans, dhole packs are bold enough to attack large and dangerous animals, such as wild boar, water buffalo, and tigers. They have great jumping and leaping abilities, being able to jump 10 to 12 feet (3—4 m) high, and leap 17 to 20 feet (5—6 m) long distances in one leap with a running start. Dholes once ranged throughout most of South, East, and Southeast Asia. Sadly, today it is the most endangered Asian predator, and only around 3,000 dholes in the world survive.

A takin female and her calf. Both sexes of the large goat-ox have horns.

SNOW LEOPARD The snow leopard is a moderately large cat native to the mountain ranges of Central and South Asia. Snow leopards show several adaptations for living in a cold mountainous environment. Their bodies are stocky, their fur is thick, and their ears are small and rounded, all of which help to minimize heat loss. Their feet are wide, which distribute their weight better for walking on snow, and cushioned furry thickenings on their paws increase their traction on steep and unstable surfaces, as well as assisting in minimizing heat loss. Snow leopards' tails are long and flexible, which helps them to maintain their balance. Their tails are also very thick due to the storage of fats, and are very thickly covered with fur which, apart from reducing heat loss, allows them to be used like a blanket to protect their faces when asleep. Snow leopards are hunted wantonly in many countries, for instance, Mongolia. They are endangered now, and their total wild population is estimated at only 3,000 to 7,000 worldwide. Happily, there has been some success with breeding snow leopards in captivity, and there are 600 to 700 snow leopards in zoos around the world.

TAKIN The takin, the national animal of Bhutan, is classified as highly vulnerable. It is a goat-antelope found in the heavily forested areas of the Eastern Himalayas. Takin stand 43 to 51 inches (110—130 cm) at the shoulder and weigh up to 2,205 pounds (1,000 kg). Its curved muzzle resembles a "bee stung moose" because of the swollen appearance of the face. They are mostly covered with thick golden wool except for black on the underbelly. Takin are maintained and preserved in a compound outside Paro.

MYTH OF THE TAKIN

Bhutan selected the takin as its national animal based both on its uniqueness and its strong association with the country's religious history and mythology. According to legend, when the lama Drukpa Kunley visited Bhutan in the 16th century, a large congregation of devotees gathered from around the countryside to witness his magical powers. The people begged the lama to perform a miracle. The saint, however, in his usual unorthodox and outrageous way, demanded that he first be served a whole cow and a goat for lunch. He devoured these animals with relish and left only their bones. After letting out a large and satisfied burp, he took the goat's head and stuck it onto the bones of the cow. Then with a snap of his fingers, he commanded the strange beast to rise up and graze on the mountainside. To the astonishment of the people, the animal arose and ran up to the meadows to graze. This animal came to be known as the takin, and to this day these animals can be seen grazing on the mountainsides of Bhutan.

NATIONAL PARKS AND RESERVES

Bhutan's history of isolation and its policy of sustainable development provide decision makers with a unique opportunity to conserve the country's natural and cultural heritage. As a first step in conserving its natural heritage, Bhutan has established a system of nine protected areas. The system sets aside some 26 percent of the country's total land area in national parks, nature reserves, wildlife sanctuaries, and conservation areas.

JIGME DORJI NATIONAL PARK This is the largest protected area in the country, encompassing 1,679 square miles (4,349 square km), covering the western parts of Paro, Thimphu, and Punakha districts, and almost all of the Gasa District. The park is the habitat of several endangered species, including the takin, blue sheep, snow leopard, musk deer, Himalayan black bear, and red panda. The road from Paro to Choolhari, Lingshi, Laya, and Gasa goes through this sheltered wild space.

ROYAL MANAS NATIONAL PARK This 395 square-mile (1,023-square km) park in south central Bhutan adjoins the Black Mountain National

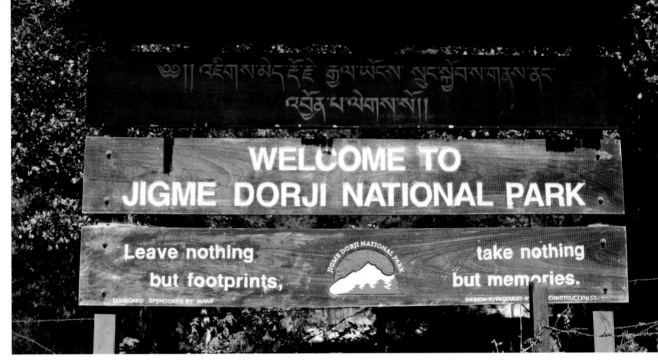

Park to the north and India's Manas Wildlife Sanctuary and Manas Tiger Reserve to the south. It was initially established as a royal hunting reserve. It is the home of rhinoceros, buffalo, tiger, leopard, gaur, bear, elephant, wild dog, pygmy hog, hispid hare, and several species of deer.

An environmentally alert sign in Jigme Dorji National Park.

JIGME SINGYE WANGCHUK NATIONAL PARK This area of 502 square miles (1,300 square km) protects the range of mountains that separate eastern and western Bhutan. Its plant life includes a large variety of broadleaf species, conifers, and alpine pastures. Animal life includes the tiger, Himalayan black bear, leopard, red panda, goral, serow, sambar, wild pig, and golden langur. The Phobjikha Valley (Gangtey), which is the winter habitat of around 260 black-necked cranes, is situated in this protected park.

THRUMSHINGLA NATIONAL PARK The 297-square mile (768-square km) Thrumshingla National Park is Bhutan's newest national park and is situated between Bumthang and Mongar. It protects temperate forests of fir and chir pine. It is known for its scenic views, dense forests, and alpine meadows. Some threatened species in this reserve include the rufous-necked hornbill, Satyra tragopan, Ward's trogon, and chestnut-breasted partridge. A small area near the Thrumshingla Pass has a natural garden established to showcase Bhutan's rhododendron diversity in their natural habitat.

The Thrumshingla Pass is the highest motorable pass in Bhutan.

BHUTANESE

Bhutanese children wearing their national costumes, following the rule of *driglam namzha*, the national practice of dress and behavior. This mandatory rule keeps traditional Bhutanese culture alive despite modern influences.

CHAPTER 6

T HE TERMS "BHUTAN" AND "Bhutanese" have been applied to the Land of the Thunder Dragon and its people by the outside world since the first non-Bhutanese visitor stepped into the rustic paradise. The origin of these terms is certainly Sanskrit, which is the origin of many northern Indian languages and the inspiration for the alphabets of Tibet and Bhutan.

Bhutan consists of a mosaic of different peoples who continue to live in remote valleys, isolated from one another and the outside world by formidable mountain passes.

Bhutanese women and their children in Tongsa. Inheritance in Bhutan generally goes in the female rather than the male line. Daughters will inherit their parents' house.

61

The likeliest of several possible interpretations is that the name "Bhutan" derives from either *bhu-utthan*, meaning highland, or from *bhotias*, referring to people from the Himalaya Mountains or Tibet.

ETHNIC GROUPS

The population may be broadly divided into three main ethnic groups—Ngalongs (also called Bhote, of Tibetan origin) in the western and central regions, Lhotshampas (of Nepalese origin) in the southern border areas, and Sharchops in the east of the country. These ethnic groups make up today's Drukpa population. There are also a number of small aboriginal tribes, making up approximately 7 percent of the entire population. They are scattered in villages throughout the country.

These basic divisions probably confuse as much as they help when it comes to understanding the differences among the peoples of Bhutan, who are referred to collectively as Drukpa in the national language of Bhutan. In reality, some of the population and some of the literature on Bhutan consider this term to apply only to the people who came from Mongolia, whereas some others feel it

A modern mother and daughter in the Chokor Valley. The slower pace of living facilitates more interaction among family members.

applies to those who came from Tibet, that is, the Ngalongs. There are still others who say the term refers only to those who belong to the Drukpa religious belief system.

This confusion arises from the close interaction between the secular and the religious in Bhutan's formative history, so that language sometimes does not distinguish clearly between secular and religious identities.

NGALONGS

Today's Ngalongs (Ngar-longs) are descendants of ninth-century immigrants from Tibet. They arrived, some 1,200 years or more ago, through the northern passes to settle in the west of what is now Bhutan. The reasons for their migration are lost in time. We know that later peoples from Tibet fled from trouble at home, so unrest might have been a factor in Bhutan's first immigration. But there is no doubt the immigrants were also attracted to the comparatively good farming areas in the uninhabited valleys of western Bhutan. The Ngalongs regard that part of Bhutan west of the Black Mountains, including Thimphu, Paro, and Ha, as their homeland.

The Ngalongs look like their Tibetan ancestors. Their language is also closely related to Tibetan, with some pronunciation and grammatical differences. It is the language of the Ngalongs, known as Dzongkha, that became the national language of Bhutan.

The Ngalongs were separated from their neighbors in central Bhutan by the Black Mountains. Peaks in the Black Mountains range between 4,900 and 8,900 feet (1,494 and 2,713 m) above sea level. Today a road twists and turns across the 10,827 feet-high (3,300 m) pass of Pele La, which joins the two parts of the country.

A Ngalong father and his sons. The Ngalongs are the descendants of Tibetans and the largest ethnic group in Bhutan.

The name Ngalong means "first to rise," indicating not that the Ngalongs rose up against any authority but that they were the first people in Bhutan to accept Buddhism.

Bhutanese boys of mixed origins playfully wearing moustaches.

LHOTSHAMPAS

The Lhotshampas (Lhot-sharm-pahs) of the southern foothills and lowlands are mostly descendants of immigrants from Nepal who settled in Bhutan between 1880 and 1960. Studies show that their migration to Bhutan was a continuation of a west-east pattern that had existed in Nepal for hundreds of years, largely driven by overpopulation and scarcity of food.

Eventually they came to the eastern border of Nepal, which was already occupied by people known as Limbus, who objected to the occupation of their traditional lands. Rather than push south into the disease-infested lowlands of Nepal, the migrants crossed the border into Sikkim and West Bengal, then moved farther into the mid-level hills of Bhutan's western regions of Ha, Samchi, Chhukha, and Daga, where they cleared the forest and established farms. As their numbers increased, they cleared new lands right up to Bhutan's southern border with India and continued in the westward movement across Bhutan.

The term Lhotshampas generally describes all people who trace their roots to Nepal. Far from being an ethnic descriptive term, it includes Aryan-featured high-caste Hindus, mostly Brahmin and Chhetri, with a minority of occupational castes, such as farmers or merchants, or low castes such as laborers and untouchables. These caste groups make up some 50 percent of the Lhotshampa population. The rest are Rai, Gurung, Limbu, and Tamang, groups that come from Nepal but are socially structured more like Ngalongs and Sharchops than higher caste Hindus. Many of these groups still speak their own languages, although those languages are gradually giving way to the dominant language of the region, Nepali.

The Brahmins who came to Bhutan were hill Brahmins as opposed to plains Brahmins. This is an important distinction. Marriage rules, more strictly enforced a century ago in Nepal than in Bhutan, prevented intermarriage between the two kinds of Brahmins (identified by their surnames). Thus hill Brahmins in Nepal could not establish meaningful links with the Brahmin communities that had lived on Nepal's flatlands for centuries, and they had to keep to the hill corridors.

A Sharchop family in the Tashigang region. The Sharchops cultivate the steep sides of these valleys in Tashigang, growing corn rather than rice as their main subsistence crop.

SHARCHOPS

The name Sharchops (Shar-khops), or the alternative Sharchopas, means "people of the east," indicating that they live in eastern and southeastern Bhutan. The environment in the east of Bhutan is less rigorous than in the west since it is warmer and has drier deep valleys. The Sharchops are regarded as the original people of Bhutan or the "first-comers," although where they came from is unknown. Their house styles vary between the typically large and solid Bhutanese dwelling and fragile bamboo huts raised on stilts.

The Sharchops are regarded as being very religious, and their settlements are dotted with small community or family temples. Sharchop women are renown for their weaving skills. They work with silk and cotton, and today a good piece of their craft work, if it is for sale, can cost hundreds of dollars in the open international market.

BHUTANESE REFUGEES IN NEPAL

Bhutanese child refugees work all day breaking rocks into gravel at the Timai refugee camp in eastern Nepal.

In 1961 the government of Bhutan launched its planned developmental projects, each consisting of significant infrastructure improvements. With most Bhutanese being self-employed farmers, however, the large-scale importing of workers from India was inevitable. This influx remained unchecked for many years, and by the 1980s, the Bhutanese government had become acutely conscious not only of rampant illegal immigration of people of Nepali origin into Bhutan but also of the total absence of integration of even long-term immigrants into the mainstream of the country. Most immigrants knew little of the culture of Bhutan, and could not understand any one of the local languages, including Dzongkha. In rural areas they remained "Nepalese" in their culture and were indistinguishable from the Nepalese in Nepal itself. The government attempted to preserve Bhutan's cultural identity by discontinuing Nepali as a subject in schools, and by requiring citizens to wear the distinctive attire of the northern Bhutanese in public places. By the 1990s, prolonged attempts to stress the majority Buddhist culture and the lack of any political representation had led to deep resentment among the ethnic Nepali community in the south. Violence erupted, and kidnappings and murders of ethnic Nepalis who did not join in the protests were perpetrated. Tens of thousands of Nepali speakers fled Bhutan to refugee camps in Nepal.

The refugee exodus that funneled as many as 100,000 southerners into India and Nepal contained all ethnic groups within the generic term Lhotshampa, although it was led by Brahmins and perhaps contained a disproportionate number of Brahmins. The proportion of southerners who fled the country is frequently placed at about 40 to 50 percent of the

Lhotshampa population. Out of this refugee population have sprung a number of insurgent groups—the Bhutan Communist Party (Marxist-Leninist-Maoist), the Bhutan Tiger Force, and the United Revolutionary Front of Bhutan. The Bhutanese security forces believe these groups are behind the wave of bombings that rocked the kingdom in the period leading up to the 2008 parliamentary elections.

Many refugees in Nepal wish to return, but talks between the governments of Nepal and Bhutan have not arrived at a solution. In the meantime, the poorer Lhotshampa farmers who stayed in Bhutan are petitioning to occupy the long-vacant lands of those who sold their farms and left the country.

The linguistically distinctive Brokpas, who are seminomadic herdsmen, live in the high valleys of Merak and Sakteng, located at the eastern tip of the country.

CENTRAL AND MARGINAL GROUPS

Many of Bhutan's ethnic groups do not fit into any of the three main categories. Several of these groups live in central Bhutan, and many speak their own languages. The Bumthaps speak Bumthangkha and occupy Bumthang, which is a group of four valleys at varying altitudes of 8,530 to 13,123 feet (2,600—4,000 m). The Khyengs live in the central-south district, which takes their name, and are known for their basketry and use of wild forest plants. Tibetans live in the north and central-west. The Lepchas, a distinctive group, see their homeland as a lost kingdom now bridging three kingdoms—the westernmost part of Bhutan, Sikkim, and the easternmost border areas of Nepal.

ONE NATION, ONE PEOPLE

Bhutan's ethnic mosaic is strongly bonded by the shared practice of Tantric Buddhism, which had its origins in Tibet but has acquired its own Bhutanese character and features. Apart from Hindus among the population in the south, Bhutanese are very devoutly Buddhist. This provides a universality of values and beliefs that overcomes particular ethnic divisions of language and

The Bhutanese authorities actively promoted intermarriage across ethnic divisions with the objective of fusing a national identity and forestalling the possibility of conflict on ethnic lines. Substantial wedding gifts were offered by the government to couples who took up the offer. As could be expected, the strict marriage rules of the Brahmins and Chhetris prevented these groups from mixing well into the officially sanctioned melting pot, but many in the lower castes saw it as a way out of a permanently humiliating social position.

physical features. It is this universality of Buddhist values that was the basis of King Jigme Singye Wangchuck's concept of "one nation, one people," onto which the modern attributes of a nation-state are constructed—a single national language, a national education, freedom to move and marry within the nation, and a single national identity.

WEALTH AND STATUS

Many foreign observers have commented on the comparative equality enjoyed by the peoples of Bhutan. None of the ethnic groups has a position of favor or superiority over others. There are no large landowners, and almost all families own enough land to meet their needs. Village headmen and local representatives to the National Assembly are elected through universal suffrage, and any adult can run for election. A small middle class of people educated in India and the West is beginning to emerge, as are differences of wealth between farmers, wage earners, and businessmen. But such degrees of wealth have not led to social separation. Rather, the opposite is true. Since Bhutan became a hereditary kingdom, serfdom and privilege of rank have been largely removed. All Bhutanese are equal under the law, and this includes the king.

The king is universally respected in Bhutan. This regard, however, does not separate him from his people. Any citizen may petition the king to redress a grievance or to request land. It is not unusual for villagers to be visited

In the early 1970s intermarriage between the Lhotshampas and the mainstream Bhutanese population was encouraged by the government as a way of integrating Bhutanese society.

THE HIERARCHY OF THE SCARVES

Bhutanese men wear scarves for all official occasions and when going to the dzong or a temple. The scarves, known as kabney (KAB-nay), are made of a light material, usually silk or cotton, and are not intended to keep a person warm but to disclose his status. A scarf is worn over the

left shoulder and draped across the body. Status is evident by the color. The majority of people wear white scarves. Saffron scarves are reserved for the je khenpo (the chief abbot of Bhutan) and the king.

Dark blue is for members of the Royal Advisory Council. Women wear a narrow red scarf that may have colored decorations and are fringed at both ends.

by their king. When he does so, nobody grovels on the ground. The king will sit on the floor among schoolchildren or farmers, sharing a family lunch or exchanging ideas. The same national dress is worn by king and commoner. There is no "high" Dzongkha language to distinguish an upper class. In the sense of symbols of social equality and equality of opportunity, Bhutan comes close to its Shangri-la image.

There are distinctions within Bhutanese society, however, as in any society, and some people are shown more respect than others. There is in fact an institutionalized hierarchy of respect evident in the Bhutanese folkways—the tradition of the scarves. Scarves of certain colors indicate the position one holds in the government. Scarves are also presented for various celebrations and as gifts.

The most warmly respected people in Bhutan are the monks who, in the daily course of their lives, handle no money and dedicate themselves to helping all humanity.

LIFESTYLE

Local artisans selling traditional Bhutanese
handicrafts at a market in Thimphu.

BHUTANESE LIFESTYLE IS determined by isolation, both from outside influence and between parts of Bhutan; the predominance of subsistence farming; and the strong attachment to Tantric Buddhism. Centuries of isolation means that local society, language, and culture shape the worldview of a Bhutanese, and meaningful social relationships are found only within each person's own valley.

Subsistence farming does not produce any great surpluses that might take a farmer to distant markets, so there is little reason to travel to

Bhutan is a unique blend of the old and the new. This country is one that is slowly opening up to the modern world in a finely-tuned balance with its ancient traditions.

Bhutanese students wearing their school uniforms in Tongsa.

them. The practice of Buddhism that the Bhutanese share does occasionally call for pilgrimages to sacred locations. For daily religious purposes, however, a farmer visits his local shrine, where he worships with family and neighbors. The Bhutanese lifestyle is essentially domestic and parochial and, for most people, it has not changed much since the country was unified in the 17th century.

WORKING WAYS

About 80 percent of Bhutanese tend the land, producing food crops. They also keep animals, not for their meat but to pull plows and carts, carry harvest produce, and provide milk and wool.

The country's population tends to be congregated in villages on fertile patches of valley land. Hundreds of years of isolation have created close-knit, self-reliant communities, where neighbors often exchange labor, working on each other's land when needed. Issues that affect the community as a whole are discussed with neighbors.

THE FAMILY

A Bhutanese family is usually large. Couples are likely to have five or six children. Although most couples are monogamous, they are prone to divorce and remarriage, resulting in what anthropologists refer to as serial polygamy. Family members living under one roof, therefore, may be from more than one biological family.

Traditional values have little to say about family structure as long as children are well looked after and the elderly are supported. Illegitimacy does not exist. Whatever their parentage, all children are recognized as equal members of the community. In households where partners have changed, children often have a choice as to where they wish to live and may choose to alternate between households.

In Bhutan the family is a social rather than a purely biological unit and may contain anybody who agrees to become part of it. By extension, a village community may be seen as one big family, with each member shouldering some responsibility for the welfare of all the others.

HOUSES

Traditional Bhutanese houses are made out of mud, bamboo, and wood. Bhutanese village houses are generally large, to accommodate an extended family, and solid, for protection against heavy rains and harsh winters. It is possible to build a house, usually two stories, in two to three weeks with the help of several families, neighbors, and friends. This is usually done during the low-activity period between planting and harvest.

In the west of the country, walls up to 3 feet (1 m) thick are made of tightly compacted mud. In the subtropical south, walls are made of wood, sometimes raised from the often muddy ground by one story on stilts.

The front door of the house traditionally opens to the south. There are few windows on the ground floor because it is commonly used for keeping animals and as a granary. Windows at the upper front are likely to be big and may be glazed or have sliding shutters.

On the upper floor is a room containing a Buddha image and offerings of flowers or fruit, where individuals or the family together may come to prostrate themselves to the Buddha and to meditate. It is in this room that guests will be received. The kitchen is also likely to be upstairs, and because of the absence of electricity, it will be the warmest room in winter, the place where the family eats and lingers until bedtime, chatting or planning the next day. Bedrooms are simple—one for each couple and their smallest children. Other children may sleep together when young but are divided according to gender once they reach puberty.

The most amazing thing about a Bhutanese traditional house is that no nails, screws, or metal hinges are used in its construction. All materials used are locally available. Shown here are tradtional buildings and terraced fields in Punakha.

Building a house is a happy occasion; people sing and dance while they work, and eat, drink, and socialize when the workday ends.

Under Bhutanese law, women are equal to men, and there is little observed gender discrimination. Bhutanese women are free to make their own mistakes and can marry for love. There is no economic basis for discrimination, since women work alongside their men in the fields and generate as much of the subsistence needs and family income as their husbands. In addition, women do much of the housework, including cooking, and most of the chores associated with raising children. Women fall behind in education, regrettably, because of the cost involved and the ongoing need to have labor on the farm. Also, the learning of Buddhist scriptures by heart does not interest them, since only boys can be ordained as monks or take vows as lay teachers. Although a high-ranking Bhutanese monk has declared, "There is no difference between the sexes on the path to enlightenment," all monks are men. Women may join an order of nuns—which has considerably lower status and influence than the monks—and are free to follow the way of the Buddha as far as they can, but a woman will never become a chief abbot.

Interestingly, Bhutanese women have traditionally had more legal rights than men in surrounding cultures, the most prominent being the presumptive right of land ownership. Inheritance in Bhutan generally is assigned in the female rather than the male line. Daughters will inherit their parents' house. A man is expected to make his own way in the world and often moves to his wife's home. The property of each extended Bhutanese family is controlled by an "anchor mother" who is assisted by the other women of the family in running household affairs. If she becomes unable to manage the property due to age or infirmity, the position of anchor mother passes to a sister, daughter, or niece.

The roof is typically made of overlapping wooden shingles. The slope of the roof is slight, enabling the placement of large rocks in rows on the shingles to keep them in place. In towns and some villages near a road, wooden shingles have been replaced with corrugated iron sheeting or slate tiles. Between the ceiling and the roof is a low attic that serves as additional storage space. Besides keeping hay, which is used to feed the animals on the lower floor, the packed attic also serves to insulate the house.

The wooden front of the house may be carved and painted with religious and folk symbols. Bhutanese believe that these emblems will invite good luck and fertility to the occupants and turn away the bad spirits that spread disharmony and disease.

Before a new house is occupied, it is blessed by monks, and a Buddhist prayer flag is placed in the center of the roof. Several other flags may flutter from bamboo poles at the sides of the house.

A traditionally painted wooden house in Paro.

BIRTH

Most births take place in the home, and any birth, whether it is a boy or a girl, is cause for ceremony and celebration. A purification ceremony (locally called a Lhabsang) has to be performed in the house on the third day after a baby is born, before the child may receive any visitors. Customarily, gifts of eggs, rice, or corn are prepared, and the newborn baby will be given some money for good luck and prosperity.

There is no rush to name the child. The parents often visit one or more reputable abbots or monks to select good, lucky names. Once an auspicious name has been decided, the child's *kye tsi* (kai-et-si) or horoscope is written based on the Bhutanese calendar.

Every new mother consumes a hot alcoholic beverage made with butter and eggs to increase her milk supply. The same drink is served to guests, and everybody is happy and full of good wishes after drinking a few cups.

The kye tsi *horoscope is drawn up with great care, based on a child's birth date according to the Bhutanese lunar calendar. It lists all the rituals the child must perform throughout his or her life in order to maintain good health and have a good life, as well as supplementary rituals that are to be performed if the child experiences problems. The* kye tsi *reflects the fatalistic attitude of most Bhutanese, although it is a source of psychological comfort when life delivers hard punches.*

A Bhutanese marriage does not involve any vows to love, honor, and obey. Sororal polygyny, a rare form of marriage, is often practiced in Bhutan, where a man marries two or more sisters. The retired previous king is married to four sisters.

PUBERTY

Bhutanese treat puberty as a natural event, and there is no special rite of passage related to puberty, as in many traditional cultures. Prepubescent sex is socially forbidden, but once puberty has arrived (often as old as 14 or 15 years of age), sexual relations and marriage in one of its forms are considered normal.

MARRIAGE

The majority of Bhutanese, who cannot afford an expensive wedding or do not want a formal ceremony, enter marriage gradually—the girl simply moves in with the boy, and nothing needs to be announced. If the arrangement does not work out, they drift apart or separate. Women as well as men have the right to decide if they wish to continue in a relationship. Society does mildly object to a wife's leaving her husband for another man, but social disapproval rarely goes beyond requiring the "other man" to pay a fine to the abandoned husband. A man may have up to three wives.

Young people today are likely to want their parents' blessing for their union. If it is not given, the couple simply confronts both families with the fait accompli of their pairing. Nobody would suggest that strangers get married, and children are not obliged to accept the choices of the parents.

A typical lavish wedding begins on a day and time set by an astrologer. Accompanied by his male friends, the bridegroom escorts the bride from her house to his house, where members of his family stand in front of the door in welcome, holding a bowl of milk and a bowl of water, symbolizing fertility and prosperity.

A line of monks will bestow ritual blessings on the couple, who exchange cups of wine as the sign of the union. Families, neighbors, and friends will present the couple with white scarves to indicate their good wishes and hand over wedding gifts, that are usually pieces of fabric presented in good-luck quantities of three, five, or seven. A feast follows, with liberal consumption of alcohol and joyful dancing.

Funeral rites are elaborate and usually held in the house for seven days.

FUNERALS

A funeral is the most important and costly of ceremonies for the Bhutanese, who believe strongly in reincarnation and therefore will take serious measures to ensure that the deceased is reborn in the most favorable circumstance.

Lamas are called to the house as soon as possible after death has occurred, where they read from the *Book of the Dead*. This book, Tibetan in origin, is a guide to the dead person's spirit through the various stages of *bardo* (BAR-do), the interval between death and reincarnation.

The deceased is cremated at an auspicious time chosen by an astrologer, normally three days after death. The corpse, placed in a fetal position, is wrapped in a white cloth, laid atop the funeral pyre, and the wood is set on fire. Everybody in the locality attends this good-bye ceremony, throwing white scarves and paper money into the flames while praying for a good reincarnation. The ashes usually are scattered in the nearest river. Prayer flags are raised to bring merit to the deceased and hasten a good rebirth.

EDUCATION AND LITERACY

Secular education was widely introduced in the 1960s. Sadly, today only 47 percent of the population is literate, and even this is badly skewed—60 percent of men are literate, versus 34 percent of women. Until the 1950s, the only formal education available to Bhutanese students, except at private schools in Ha and Bumthang, was through Buddhist monasteries. Lessons are taught in English, with Dzongkha being taught as a second language.

Virtually the same subjects that are taught in Western schools are offered in Bhutan. The educational system consists of one year of preprimary school, five years of primary school, three years of junior high school, and three years of high school. Higher education, which is provided by the Royal University of Bhutan, was established in 2003. It has a number of specialized colleges, including the Jigme Namgyel Polytechnic (which used to be the Royal Bhutan Polytechnic) and Sherubtse College in Kanglung (which had been a junior college). Kharbandi Technical School in Kharbandi, Chhukha District, was also important.

Students in a class. The full curriculum—which covers two languages, agriculture, geography, history, Bhutanese traditions, environment, population, science, morals, health, and hygiene—typifies Bhutan's perception of its needs in the years ahead.

HEALTH

Today Bhutan has one of the best-organized primary health-care systems in the region. Even as a late starter in modern health care, Bhutan has managed to cover over 90 percent of its population with basic medical service, despite the extremely difficult terrain with scattered and inaccessible residents. The focus of the public health sector has been to increase the accessibility of such care. A network of Basic Health Units covers the country now, and basic service and essential drugs are provided free of charge to all patients.

A young woman receiving a steam treatment at a clinic in Bhutan. Health care in Bhutan is made up of an interesting blend of traditional allopathic remedies and modern medicine. Treatment is often targeted at body as well as soul, and this sometimes requires the exorcising of evil spirits that may be lodged in the body.

Each unit is staffed by a health assistant, who is trained to diagnose problems, provide treatment, and refer the more seriously ill to a doctor at a small district hospital; a nurse or midwife, who among other duties assists in difficult cases of childbirth and keeps accurate records of causes of illness and death. Also on hand is a basic health worker to assist the doctor and the nurse. The team makes a regular circuit tour to provide health care at centers in remote locations.

Cases that cannot be treated at the district level due to limited staff and facilities are referred to one of the three larger hospitals, the best of which is in Thimphu. Alternatively, the very sick living nearer a better medical center in India may have their transportation to that center and their treatment there arranged and paid for by the government.

The great advantages of modern medicine have not closed the door on traditional medicine, particularly guidelines on what foods to eat or to avoid, herbal potions, and occasionally, acupuncture.

RELIGION

Young monks taking a breather in front of the
Karchu Dratsang Monastery in Bumthang.

TODAY FREEDOM OF RELIGION IS guaranteed in Bhutan. As part of this freedom, it is forbidden to persuade or force people to change religions, although individuals may change if they wish. It is estimated that between two-thirds and three-quarters or more of the population is Tantric Buddhist.

About one-quarter to one-third are practitioners of Hinduism. The remainder includes some small pockets of the Bon religion (the original animistic belief system of the Himalayas), some syncretic (blended

Part of the Drukpa school of Mahayana Buddhism in Bhutan, the Punakha Dzong is located at the confluence of the Pho Chhu (father) and Mo Chhu (mother) rivers in the Punakha-Wangdü Valley.

The constitution of Bhutan states that "a Bhutanese citizen shall have the right to freedom of thought, conscience, and religion." The government, however, restricts this right in practice by barring non-Buddhist missionaries from entering the country, limiting construction of non-Buddhist religious buildings, and restraining the celebration of some non-Buddhist religious festivals.

A devotee turning the prayer wheels in a Buddhist temple inThimphu.

of several beliefs) religions among noncaste groups in the south, and a small number of Christians. The Bon religion in Tibet and Bhutan has shamanistic elements. Shamans, in the Bon religion, are intermediaries who communicate between humans and the spiritual world.

TANTRIC BUDDHISM

Buddhism, as it is understood and practiced in Bhutan, is considered the final manifestation of the religion's long evolution. The name Tantric refers to the tantras, a large body of ancient scriptures that are thought to have been produced between the 3rd and 10th centuries. Tantric Buddhism forms part of the "larger vehicle" (Mahayana) of Buddhist thought, in the sense of recognizing more scriptures and providing an enlarged role for the lamas. It includes all the basic truths as set out by the Buddha Gautama. The other main branch of Buddhist thought is called Theravada or Hinayana, meaning the "little vehicle," which recognizes only the original Buddhist scriptures. Tantric Buddhism is also referred to in some of the literature as Vajrayana, the Diamond Vehicle. Like all forms of Buddhism, it originated in India, but the Diamond Vehicle disappeared from India following the Muslim invasions in the 13th century.

BELIEFS

Bhutan is the only country in the world with the Tantric form of Mahayana Buddhism as its official religion.

The fundamental beliefs of Tantric Buddhism parallel those of Theravada Buddhism. The Buddha proclaimed the absence of any god or supreme beings and replaced the idea of deity with the philosophy of cause and effect—that the consequence of actions in previous lives obliges all life forms to reincarnate forever, until and unless the release from the cycle of rebirth is achieved through enlightenment, when all desire and suffering—which accompanies all existence—is extinguished in the void of Nirvana.

BUDDHISM: THE SHARED BASIC BELIEFS

All types of Buddhism and all sects agree on the basic principles of the belief system as given around 560 B.C. in sermons by Sakyamuni Buddha (also called Gautama) on the India-Nepal border. These basic tenets are:

THE FOUR NOBLE TRUTHS

1. *Human life is full of suffering.*
2. *People create this suffering because they are afraid to let go—they grasp after the temporary pleasures of happiness and life.*
3. *If people stop grasping and trying to possess what gives them pleasure and avoid what gives them pain, suffering will cease.*
4. *Following the noble Eightfold Path will help people let go and lead them eventually to the end of suffering.*

THE NOBLE EIGHTFOLD PATH

1. *RIGHT VIEWS—think positively of the good in oneself and in other people.*
2. *RIGHT THOUGHTS—care for others, be sympathetic and understanding.*
3. *RIGHT SPEECH—do not lie or say hurtful or stupid things.*
4. *RIGHT ACTION—do not kill, injure, or steal.*
5. *RIGHT LIVELIHOOD—in your work do not cheat anyone or cause harm.*
6. *RIGHT EFFORT—make the effort needed to follow the eightfold path.*
7. *RIGHT MINDFULNESS—be aware of your thoughts and actions.*
8. *RIGHT CONTEMPLATION—be peaceful in your mind.*

THE FIVE PRECEPTS

These are the Buddha's five rules for everyday life:

1. *Be sympathetic and helpful to all living things, and do not harm or kill them.*
2. *Do not steal or take what is not given freely by others, and be generous to the needy.*
3. *Never take more than you need.*
4. *Do not tell lies or say bad things about others.*
5. *Never act thoughtlessly or carelessly.*

In Tantric Buddhism great attention is focused on the teacher (or lama), whose interaction with laymen is necessary to an understanding of the tantras, and on ritual practice and meditation as paths toward enlightenment. As such, the recitation of mantras, the turning of prayer wheels, the raising of prayer flags, prostrations to the Buddha, and the creation and use of mandalas (symbolic paintings on paper and in sand) can help a believer achieve his true goal in life, which is not to live longer and get richer but rather to advance toward enlightenment.

BON

Bon was an ancient religion that existed throughout the Himalayas before Buddhism arrived in Bhutan in the seventh century. Mostly because Buddhism does not prohibit the simultaneous embrace of two (or more) religions, Bon beliefs and practices became fused with Buddhism.

Certain warlike Bon deities are thought to be predecessors of the pantheon of deities associated with Tantric Buddhism, and some of them are bloodthirsty in appearance. Such "Buddhist gods" take on this visage to scare away evil spirits—precisely what the old Bon gods did to help its followers. Likewise, the Bon practice of praying to their gods to bring rain, cure illness, overcome poverty, and obtain objects of desire continues today,

A death dancer frightens off evil spirits at a harvest festival in Sakteng.

although this has nothing at all to do with Buddhist thought. Prayers are offered to the Buddha, to the bodhisattvas (beings that help others attain Nirvana), and to a variety of deities, requesting intervention in material life and promising offerings if successful.

Another vestige of the Bon religion is the significance that Bhutanese place on mountains and lakes. Some mountains are considered sacred, so mortal man cannot set foot on the higher elevations or stand on the summits without risking dire consequences. In the Bon religion, ravens are also sacred.

CHRISTIANITY

There are some 6,000 Christians in Bhutan, about 2 percent of the population. Most are uneducated and from the poorer classes. Christianity is not recognized by the government and is not mentioned with other religions on their official website. Although the Bible has been translated into the national language, Dzongkha, and into Nepalese, there is little formal Christian teaching. It is against the law to build a church, so services are held in private homes. The government seems to fear that Christians will cause tensions in society between people of different faiths.

DAILY PRACTICE

Bhutanese farmers need no intellectual rationalization of their religion. They are born Buddhist and adopt without question the beliefs and practices of their family and community. They have a duty to respect and assist monks and religious teachers and to lead life in such a way as to gain merit and thereby be reincarnated at a higher level of awareness.

Bhutanese adhere strictly to Buddha's commandments, the chief of which is not to kill. They do not hunt or fish or kill their farm animals. If such animals die of old age, fall off a cliff, or are on sale at the market when dead, however, they may be eaten. Buddhists also have a duty to perform daily and special-occasion rituals and to participate in the religious festivals that constantly punctuate Bhutanese life.

Tantric practices require them to repeat daily prayers and make offerings at the altar inside their home, visit temples, or *ihakhangs* (i-hak-khang), on special occasions, give to monks, lamas, and monasteries, encourage at least one son to enter monkhood, light butter lamps in homage, make pilgrimages to holy places, arrange appropriately elaborate rituals on the occasions of birth and death, erect prayer flags, and take part in communal prayers.

A Buddhist family altar in a farmhouse in Paro. Bhutanese worship the Buddha, Guru Rimpoche, and all the deities of the Tantric and Bon pantheon. Such worship is also extended to the religious masters.

THE OFFICIAL RELIGION

The special role religious masters have in Tantric Buddhism has led to many different schools of thought, each following the particular interpretations or teachings of a master. All masters recognize the basic principles of Buddhist dogma, and because of the built-in tolerance of Buddhism, which allows Buddhists to belong to other religions and practice any of the "many paths to Enlightenment," no conflict arises between the schools of thought. Currently, the official or national religion of Drukpa (dragon sect) coexists with Nyingmapa (the oldest sect of Mahayana Buddhism, popularly known as the Vajrayana), which was the sect founded by the revered Guru Rimpoche and is believed by scholars to be the earliest expression of Tibetan Tantric Buddhism.

The Drukpa school was founded in Tibet by Tsangpa Gyare Yeshe Dorje (1161—1211), whose teachings were introduced to western Bhutan in 1222 by Phajo Drugom Shigpo. The Drukpa school's influence spread throughout the land after Shabdrung Ngawang Namgyal unified the country under a system of government that gave full power to the Drukpas.

The traditional silver bell, the *drilbu*, representing wisdom, and the *dorje*, representing compassion and power, are used in the numerous Buddhist rituals of Bhutan.

THE DIAMOND-THUNDERBOLT

The *dorje* (dor-jay), or the diamond-thunderbolt, looks like a baby's rattle. Four or eight prongs branch out in two directions from the center of an axis, curl around and join together again at either end. It is also known by the Sanskrit term *vajra* (vaj-rah), meaning "diamond."

The diamond-thunderbolt is very symbolic and is also the most important of the many ritual objects associated with Tantric Buddhism. The belief is that diamonds and thunderbolts represent purity and indestructibility, and together they stand for knowledge and the male element.

To an outsider, some imagination may be needed to visualize a diamond and a thunderbolt in this ritual object. To a Bhutanese, however, it is quite

Tantric Buddhism sees knowledge (the body of consciously recognized fact) as male in essence. Wisdom (appropriate use of knowledge) is female. Knowledge by itself is static, and wisdom by itself has no meaning. To progress along the path toward the sublime state of Enlightenment requires union of knowledge and wisdom.

For this reason, Tantric divinities are often represented in sexual union. Just as life cannot continue without man and woman, life (which is suffering) cannot be extinguished without fusing the male and female. Male and female divisions, like all relative truth, cease to exist when their nature is perfectly understood. If this begins to sound a little confusing, it may explain why Tantric Buddhism places such emphasis on the interaction between a religious master and his disciple.

clear. In rituals the *dorje* is often combined with a bell known as *drilbu* (drill-boo), which represents wisdom and the female element. The *dorje* was Guru Rimpoche's weapon; with it he subdued demons, converted them, and then made them build temples.

DAGGERS AND SACRIFICES

In Hindu and Bon pre-Buddhist religions, animal sacrifice was practiced. In Buddhism, however, the taking of a life is strictly forbidden. Tantric Buddhism replaces animal sacrifice with sacrificial figurines originally made of rice dough and butter that are molded into various shapes, depending on the preferences of a particular deity, and are colorfully decorated. Today some are made permanent by using ingredients like beeswax or other sculpting material or carved from wood. Known as *tormas* (tor-mars), these inedible figures form part of every ceremony and are placed on the altar in the same way human and animal offerings were made in pre-Buddhist times.

The same procedure is followed for demons. At any ritual of purification where misfortune is blamed on evil spirits or where spiritual protection is essential, sacrificial ritual daggers, known as *phurpa* (pur-pah), are commonly used—not to kill the demons but to liberate them from their evil bodies and send them on the way to a better rebirth.

Tantric Buddhism recognizes bodhisattvas (bod-hi-sat-vahs)—enlightened beings who have progressed to the point of Nirvana but decline it in order to be reborn and help others toward that goal.

Prayer flags rustle and flutter throughout Bhutan. They may be any or all of the five colors—blue, green, red, yellow, and white—representing respectively water, wood, fire, earth, and iron. Traditionally, flags are long strips of narrow cloth block-printed in repeated patterns with texts that invoke protection and blessing from the deities. These flags are mounted longwise (so the narrow piece flutters) on tall poles and set around houses, on mountain ridges, in temple courtyards, and anywhere anybody thinks they are needed. Like the spinning prayer wheel, the fluttering flags send their messages out into the cosmos, spreading the word and building merit for all beings, not just for the one who raises the flag.

LAMAS

The term "lama" has a broader meaning than simply "monk." It refers to a religious master and teacher. It is an honorary title of address that implies knowledge and wisdom about religion, as well as a religious status in society. The title is not in itself inherited but is often transmitted from father to son along with the role of religious teacher. It applies to any of the following:

GELONG (ge-long) Ordained monks who live in monasteries or *dzongs*, wear dark red robes, take the full range of vows, and renounce sex and marriage, are called *gelong*. Most enter a monastery at between 6 and 10 years of age, an act that brings great merit to the donor family and provides the boy with what until recently would have been his only chance of an education.

At any one time there are around 7,000 monks active in Bhutan, just over 1 percent of the entire population, or 2 percent of males. Most of these belong to the official Drukpa sect, but there are also *gelong* of the Nyingmapa. Monks take a progression of vows between novice status and the fully ordained. In addition to celibacy, they are required to abstain from alcohol, tobacco, and other drugs. While some extremes of long, silent practice of meditation are known, they are not the norm. Should they find the vows too demanding, or as more often happens, they wish to quit to get

There are 22 nunneries in Bhutan, and they come under the umbrella of the Bhutan Nuns' Foundation, which was started in 2009. Many girls and women in Bhutan enter nunneries for short to long periods to gain an education and to escape poverty and abuse. The Bhutan Nuns' Foundation patron is Her Majesty the Queen Mother Ashi Tshering Yangdon Wangchuck.

married, they can buy themselves out of their vows. They are then no longer entitled to the title of *gelong* and are known by another title, which nevertheless still carries respect.

TULKU (tool-khoo) Those who can trace their line of descent through reincarnation from a great master (all in the line bear the same name, although they may not be linked by blood ties) are known as *tulkus* and are addressed as *rimpoche* (great precious one). Once a man is declared a *tulku*, he remains one whatever he does. Thus there are *tulkus* fully ordained and *tulkus* who lead a normal family life.

An older lama guiding his young disciples at the Karchu Dratsang Monastery,

GOMCHENS (gom-chens) *Gomchens* marry, have families, and go about their daily lives when they are not performing ceremonies for others, usually in return for small payments. They play an important role in isolated villages where no fully ordained monk may be available. Their religious garment is a dark red cloak that resembles that of a monk. They sometimes wear their hair long in a ponytail. Most *gomchens*, but not all, belong to the Nyingmapa.

LANGUAGE

Friends enjoying a chat on their way home.

GIVEN THE GEOGRAPHIC ISOLATION of many of Bhutan's highland villages, it is not surprising that a number of different dialects have survived. The language of the monasteries, and therefore of education, was classical Tibetan, known as Chhokey (Cho-kay). None of the languages had a written form until the 20th century.

Since the 1960s, the national language, Dzongkha, is written using the Chhokey script only. English is widely used, particularly in the educational system. Ngalopkha, also derived from Tibetan, is spoken in

There are almost as many languages spoken in Bhutan as there are ethnic groups, and often language or dialect differs significantly between neighboring valleys.

Girls learning Dzongkha in school. Equal educational opportunities exist for women, although their literacy rate is much lower than for men.

western Bhutan. Sharchopkha, an Indo-Mongolian language, is the dominant language in eastern Bhutan. Nepali is spoken in the south.

CHHOKEY

Chhokey was the lingua franca of the religious authorities of a huge area that stretched from Mongolia and Tibet to the Himalayan kingdoms of Bhutan, Ladakh, Nepal, and Sikkim. Classified linguistically as Tibeto-Burman, Chhokey is thought to have been devised in the seventh century and was in widespread use by the eighth century. As a written system for classical Tibetan, it represents an adaptation of a seventh-century alphabet from northern India that is no longer in use. It reads from left to right, has 30 consonants and 4 vowels. Corresponding to Dzongkha, Tibetan is a two-tone language, and the correct pronunciation of a syllable required memorization, which was the usual mode of learning in the monasteries.

LANGUAGES OF BHUTAN

Four main language groups exist—Dzongkha in the west and north, Bumthangkha in the central region, Sharchopkha in the east, and Nepali in the south. The first three of these each have regional dialects, and the fourth is a common language spoken by various groups that migrated to Bhutan from Nepal in the early 20th century. Some of these groups have their own languages, which are not dialects of Nepali. The Tamang, for example, live in the south and can speak Nepali as well as Tamang, a language nearer to Tibetan and Dzongkha than Nepali. In addition, English is widely used, especially in the educational system and government.

BHUTANESE PROVERBS

In the Dzongkha language there is an interesting reservoir of proverbs for every culture and every situation. The following are some of them:

- *If the thought is good, (your) place and path are good; if the thought is bad, (your) place and path are bad.*

- *The stripes of a tiger are on the outside; the stripes (character) of a person are on the inside. (A person's character cannot be told by his or her appearance.)*

- *Whatever joy you seek, it can be achieved by yourself; whatever misery you seek, it can be found by yourself.*

- *If there is no financial involvement between relatives, the relationship is harmonious.*

- *Walking slowly, even the donkey will reach Lhasa. (With enough patience and determination, even a fool will eventually reach the goal.)*

DZONGKHA

The official language, Dzongkha, is the mother tongue of the Ngalong people of the Thimphu valley and western Bhutan. English was used mainly in the south, whereas Dzongkha was little known until its use expanded in schools in the 1990s. Gradually Dzongkha spread throughout the country and became the national language. Although English is the primary medium of instruction in all schools, Dzongkha continues to be taught. The government sees the national language as a means of preserving Bhutan's culture and strengthening its national identity.

In October 2005 an internal Microsoft recommendation blocked the term "Dzongkha" from all company software and promotional material, substituting the term "Tibetan-Bhutan" instead. The International Campaign for Tibet cites the memo as stating that the use of Dzongkha "implies affiliation with the Dalai Lama, which is not acceptable to the government of China." The Bhutanese, who have never been in the domain of the Dalai Lamas, even though they revere the 14th Dalai Lama, were dismayed by the decision.

VERBAL COMMUNICATION

As in any language, Dzongkha or the other languages spoken in Bhutan, including English, have usages that are characteristic to the country. In Bhutan it is always important to show respect to the person being spoken to, so it is considered rude to speak loudly and polite to use the particle *la* at the end of a phrase or sentence, particularly an order, to soften the tone. This use of the *la* particle is often carried over into English—as in "Shut the door-la."

NONVERBAL COMMUNICATION

As elsewhere in South and Southeast Asia, body language is as important as words in expressing respect and good manners. Heads are sacred, and feet are considered to be the dirtiest part of the body. Whether sitting in a modern armchair or on the floor, feet should be tucked out of the way and should not point at anyone, and shoes are removed when visiting a home or a temple.

Homage is shown to very important religious figures in the same way as to the Buddha, by making three full prostrations, with the prostrator's head placed each time at the level of the religious master's feet.

Demonstrating good manners is important for both host and guest when invitations are made to visit a private home.

Bhutanese consider a clear "no" to be too blunt for good manners. Thus they have perfected various ways of saying yes, which vary from full agreement, through "I'm not sure," to the full meaning of no, which is likely to be expressed with nothing stronger than "Perhaps" or "We'll see."

EXCHANGING PRESENTS

Bhutanese exchange presents as a form of etiquette. A present is never opened in public or in the presence of the person giving it. To do otherwise would be worse than bad manners—it could imply that the recipient wants more of the same, or it might indicate a lack of material well-being of the giver. Gifts between equals are always reciprocated. When a gift is of significant value and comes from a person of high status, however, it is reciprocated with loyalty and service rather than with a gift.

At important events, such as birth, marriage, getting a good job or an award, and going abroad, the traditional present is cloth. The status of the donor would be evident in the number of pieces given. Money put in an envelope may be used as a substitute, along with the obligatory white scarf. The symbolic value of the scarf is of vital importance when visiting *dzongs*, monasteries, or taking part in official ceremonies.

UGEN TENZIN TSHONGKANG
'Ready made garments for Monks'

Both English and Dzongkha are used on signboards, posters, and advertisements seen everywhere in the country.

NAMES

A few weeks after a baby is born, the parents seek out a monk to name the child. The monk gives two names to every child, whether girl or boy. Very few Bhutanese names are gender-specific, thus it is usually impossible to tell the gender of a person by looking at his or her name without a title affixed.

Except for the royal family, Bhutanese have only the names given by a religious person. There are no family names. The two given names will be different, and there is no fixed position for a name. Dorji, for example, can be a person's first or second name. It is normal to address a person by first name or by both names, but not by second name alone.

There are only some 50 Bhutanese names in existence, and almost all of them originate from Tibetan. Among the most common names are Dorji and Wangchuck, the two family names of Bhutanese royalty, which can be used by anybody as personal names without in any way hinting at a royal link. Women keep their names after marriage.

People of Nepali ancestry in the south also do not have family names. If they are high-caste Hindus, however, they use one of the names belonging to their caste group, and this is passed on within the family. Nepali of lower classes generally use their ethnic group name in place of a family name—all Rais are called Rai, Limbus are called Limbu (or its equivalent), Tamangs are called Tamang, and Gurungs are called Gurung.

TITLES

Any Bhutanese of high status is addressed by his or her title, followed by first name or both names. Following are commonly used titles in Bhutan:

- Dasho *refers to a male member of the royal family, to those who have been honored by the king with the red scarf, and by polite extension, to senior government officials.*
- Ashi *is used with a female member of the royal family.*
- Lyonpo *is reserved for government ministers.*
- Lopon *is used when speaking to a senior monk.*
- Rimpoche *is used when addressing a reincarnated lama.*
- Anim *is used when speaking to a nun.*
- Aap *is used when speaking to a man (equal).*
- Busu *is used for a boy.* Am *is used for an older woman.* Bum *is used for a girl.*

Aapa, Ama, Alou, *and* Bumo *are used, respectively, for men, women, boys, and girls, of unknown name, for instance, restaurant staff.*

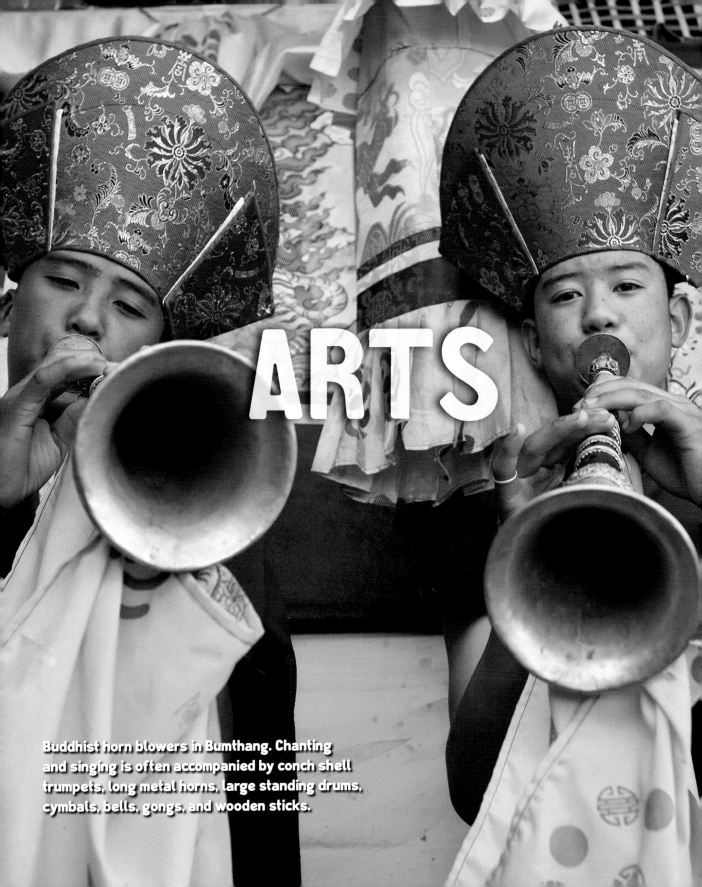

ARTS

Buddhist horn blowers in Bumthang. Chanting and singing is often accompanied by conch shell trumpets, long metal horns, large standing drums, cymbals, bells, gongs, and wooden sticks.

CHAPTER 10

BHUTANESE ART IS CHARACTERIZED by consistency in mode, its religious or folk content, and its significant Tibetan influence. Form and essence have remained practically unchanged over hundreds of years, making art literally timeless. The characteristic theme of most representational art, dance-drama, and music is the eternal struggle between good and evil.

The first School of Bhutanese Arts and Crafts was opened in 1680 under the so-called orders of Desi Shabdrung Ngawang Namygal, who had probably been dead for 31 years at the time!

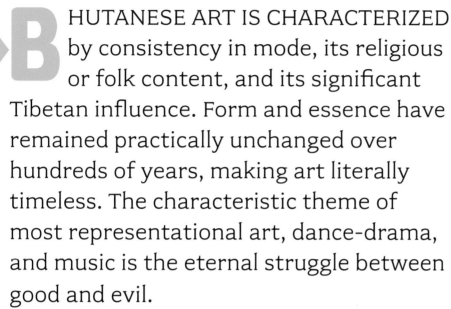
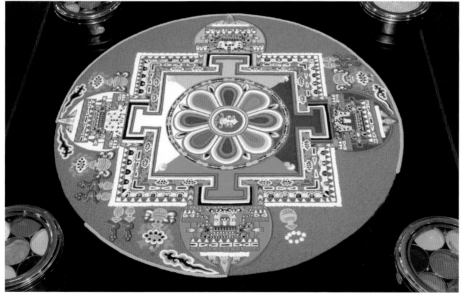

Buddhism is a major source of inspiration for Bhutanese art. Mandalas, which are schematized representations of the cosmos in Hindu and Buddhist iconography, are a favorite art form and they adorn the walls and ceilings of most *dzongs*.

Colorful local handicrafts at a market in Paro, often the products of many hands on a single object.

Artwork is usually anonymous, although significant sponsors are often named. Often a work of art is a collective achievement of several artists working together, either all at once, or one after the other. It may be a group of people decorating the front of a house with carvings and paintings, two monks painting a mandala, a troop of monks dancing and playing music, or apprentices roughing out the work for the master to add the finishing touches.

DANCE-DRAMAS

Classical dancing by lamas, known as *chham* (charm), has changed little, if at all, since this form of dance was established in the 15th century. Such dance-dramas take place during *tsechus* (JHE-choos), festivals that celebrate and instruct on the history, myths, and morality of Bhutan.

There are two types of mask dances in Bhutan—the Boe-*chham* is performed by laymen, whereas the Gyalong-*chham* is danced by the monks, wearing spectacular costumes of silk brocade. They may also wear heavy masks that represent animals, deities, one of the manifestations of Guru Rimpoche, the Buddhist teacher, or historical and mythical personages. Each drama is a story about the destruction of evil.

THE DANCE OF THE TERRIFYING DEITIES

In this very dramatic dance, which is full of symbolism, the dancers who represent deities capture in a box those dancers representing malevolent spirits. Then Guru Rimpoche, taking on his manifestation as Dorji Drakpo (fierce thunderbolt), sacrifices the spirits with a phurpa (ritual dagger), thereby saving the world from the evil spirits and, at the same time, saving the spirits from themselves.

THE DANCE OF THE NOBLEMEN AND THE LADIES

Two princes go off to war, leaving their intended princesses in the care of an old lady. No sooner are they out of sight than clowns enter and frolic with the princesses and corrupt the old woman. When the princes return, they are shocked to witness such behavior. As a punishment, they cut off the noses of the princesses and the old lady. After the weeping women repent, however, the princes call a doctor to put their noses back on. In the case of the old lady, who smells so bad that the doctor cannot approach her, the operation has to be performed with a long stick. In the end the princes marry the princesses and live happily ever after.

Professional dancers perform secular folk dances in between the more serious dramas. Most of the dancers are women, who sing while moving in circles and lines, forming and reforming patterns with intricate steps and graceful arm movements to the accompaniment of flutes, a seven-stringed lute, a two-stringed violin, and drums. Nepali dances, with their fast-stepping rhythms, are also performed at the *tsechus* of the south.

A Bhutanese musician playing a dramgyan lute, which is one of the many lyrical Tibetan musical instruments.

SONGS AND MUSIC

Songs are part and parcel of collective work or celebrations—women pounding the thick earthen walls when building a house, people in a line planting rice, or a village gathering to celebrate a wedding. Songs about formal subjects are usually sung in classical Tibetan, whereas those about secular life are sung in the everyday language of the singer or singers.

Music plays an important role, too, in religious ceremonies. Common instruments include long telescopic "Alpine" horns, oboes, double-sided drums, cymbals, trumpets, conch shells, and small bells.

A kind of popular music, heavily influenced by popular tunes from Tibetan and Hindi movies, is attracting the young Bhutanese.

PAINTING

Bhutanese religious painting has remained true to its form over many centuries, and there is very little room for individual expression. Nonetheless, the traditional style became more ornate as Chinese influences from the 17th century were manifested. Gold paint is lavishly applied, and Chinese landscapes are common subjects. Most colors are traditionally mixed from natural materials—earth, minerals, and vegetable matter—although chemical dyes have been introduced recently. Brushes are still made from animal hair tied to twigs of wood. Most colors are applied in a set order and with consideration as to what they represent.

Wall paintings and *thangkas* are the most spectacular examples of Bhutanese painting. A wall painting in a monastery is likely to be sponsored by a lay person who often specifies the main person or deity and the scene to be painted, leaving little room for spontaneity. The paint may be applied directly to sanded pressed mud or onto thin layers of cloth glued to the wall with a paste that repels insects.

Before any painting begins, the composition is sketched on the wall with great care. Proportions must be correct. Sometimes a master artist will make the preparations, leaving the painting to apprentices, then returning to apply the finishing touches. If there is a name associated with the work, it will be that of the sponsor or *jinda* (jin-dar), not the artist or artists. The inner walls of *dzongs* and temples, or *ihakhangs* (i-hak-khang), are usually covered with such paintings. Only a few original images have survived across the centuries because of the practice of repainting over the same walls, which is regarded as an act of merit.

A *thangka* is a cotton cloth stretched on a wooden frame, primed with lime and glue, and then painted. The imagery might represent a Buddha, a deity, or a geometric mandala. Even a small *thangka*, with very fine lines and gilding, can take many days to complete. After being taken from its frame, the *thangka* is appliquéd to a brocade cloth, with borders showing all around, and then affixed to wooden sticks at the top and bottom to allow hanging. When not on display, a *thangka* usually is rolled up like a scroll and protected from the light.

Amazing attention to detail is apparent in this wall painting in a Bhutanese temple.

Masked dances and dance-dramas are customary features at festivals, usually accompanied by traditional music. Energetic dancers, wearing colorful wooden or composition face masks and stylized costumes, depict heroes, demons, death heads, animals, gods, and caricatures of townspeople. The dancers preserve ancient folk and religious customs and perpetuate the ancient lore and art of mask making. Dancers enjoy royal patronage.

Craftsmen painstakingly adding color to their intricate creations carved on the wooden balustrades of the Punakha Dzong.

SCULPTURE AND CARVING

Three-dimensional sculpture in Bhutan is limited to the creation of the Buddha or deity images. An image begins as a wooden inner framework that is wrapped around with a piece of cloth onto which prayers have been written or painted. Clay is applied to this frame, and then, when dry, it is completely painted. Metal images are also made, usually by beating metal sheets into the desired shape and connecting the parts with rivets and gilding. Both clay and metal images may be set with semiprecious stones and have ornately inscribed or carved bases, often in the form of lotus buds and flowers.

Bhutanese wood carving also depicts Buddhas and deities, and some of the best work is to be seen on wooden book covers. Carving on slate flagstones is a finely developed art in Bhutan, where the handy availability of slate, and its use in the *dzongs,* make it a natural choice of medium. Bhutan's artisans are also well known for their highly skillful wooden carvings, which embellish pillars and window frames in monasteries, offices, and public buildings.

A chorten (CHOR-ten) is a material reminder of the mind of the Buddha and as such must be treated with the fullest respect. Usually known in English by the Sanskrit term stupa, a chorten is a "repository"—the first one contained the relics of the Lord Buddha. Building a chorten is similar to creating a Buddha or deity image. Ranging from as small as 7 feet (2 m) to over 33 feet (10 m) in height, there are over 10,000 chortens in Bhutan, located mainly on high mountain passes, on roads, practically everywhere. A "tree of life" covered in prayers forms the center, religious objects are sealed up inside, and the completed chorten, looking like a smoothly shaped hillock with parasols on top, is consecrated by the monks' blessings. The principles of construction and respect remain the same, regardless of whether the chorten is big or little. The fact that there may be treasures sealed inside, perhaps museum-quality pieces, creates a temptation—but any desecration of a chorten would mortally prejudice the reincarnation prospects of the despoiler.

ARCHITECTURE

Bhutanese architecture is identifiable all over the world because of the impressive photographs of the *dzongs*. The fact that few tourists are allowed access to the *dzongs* and monasteries helps to maintain the mystique of these great works of architecture. Each valley in Bhutan expresses its own architectural quality in terms of the type of building material used, ranging from mud to stone, and the special ambience of its most famous monasteries and *dzongs*.

More accessible are the traditional Bhutanese houses and the *chortens*, which are found everywhere. Influenced by an Asian tradition that stretches from Tibet to Japan, straight lines predominate in these stupas, or shrines, and walls tend to taper and slope inward toward the top. A single, big, ornate door is often the only way into a building, emphasizing the air of secrecy and forbidden interiors. Carving plays an important role in Bhutanese architecture, and nonreligious designs and representations can be found carved and painted on the front of many traditional houses.

Monks at a monastery in the Phobjika Valley. Traditional architectural designs are prevalent throughout Bhutan, especially in the form of monasteries and *dzongs*.

DZONGS

The first system of defensive fortresses known as *dzongs* was introduced in the 12th century by Gyelwa Lhanangpa, a monk from Dresung in Tibet. Later development of the sheltering *dzongs* was taken over by the remarkable Shabdrung Ngawang Namgyal in the 17th century. These formidable buildings played a role in repulsing Tibetan and Mongolian invasions. Arms captured over three centuries ago are kept to this day as trophies in the *dzongs*. Idyllically set in Bhutan's green and pleasant valleys—or perched romantically on rugged ridges, clinging to the side of a vertical cliff, or between fast-flowing rivers—these fort-like strongholds rise up from the ground as if carved from a single huge rock. Such defensive *dzongs* contained everything important that an attacker might want to possess or destroy—the ruling families, the administrative offices and records, the monastery, a large granary, and systems of access to underground water. In the event of a siege, the *dzong* could also provide sanctuary to many of the farming families in the district.

The oldest *dzongs* are built in a style reflecting the political philosophy of their time and region. In some *dzongs* the walls surround a large courtyard from which a central commanding tower rises up above the outer walls, monks' quarters, and administrative offices. In others, the central tower cuts the *dzong* into two equal parts and two courtyards—one owned by the clergy, the other by the temporal authority. Other *dzongs* follow neither of these patterns and are built to accommodate the rugged terrain on which they stand.

The inside walls of *dzongs* and monasteries and the great doors are richly decorated with paintings and slate engravings, and on festive days are backdrops for the artistic treasures brought out only for short periods on special occasions. Like the traditional houses found in any Bhutanese village, *dzongs* and monasteries are constructed without the use of nails or metal hinges. With their painted frescoes of protective deities, their grandeur and majesty, *dzongs* encapsulate Bhutanese culture. Any Bhutanese stepping into this environment becomes a part of it, aided in this integration by the wearing of the national costume and the status scarf.

A detail of an elaborately decorated window in the monastic quarter of Punakha Dzong.

WEAVING

Bhutanese textiles have only recently reached the outside world and have made such an impression that demand by far exceeds supply, sending prices through the roof. The quality of weaving is among the world's highest. For a single excellent piece of fabric of blanket length, a price exceeding twice the Bhutanese per capita annual income of $1,321 (2006 estimate) would not be unusual. Nevertheless, the Bhutanese have not forsaken the land to go into commercial fabric production. Weaving remains a spare-time household activity. Weaving in available time, each male member of the family is assured a beautiful *gho* (GOH) and the female members a *kira* (KI-rah), the traditional national costumes. There is little thought of selling to the tiny tourist market that as yet is unseen by most Bhutanese.

Cloth is highly valued in Bhutan. Traditional gifts at funerals and other occasions are pieces of cloth, given in uneven numbers. The more cloth given, the higher the status of the giver. Status has a lot to do with weaving. Bhutanese will use part of their tiny annual income to buy silk from Vietnam, China, or India that can be woven together with cotton thread to make a

Traditional weavers at work on their backstrap looms in Thimphu.

richer cloth. The most remarkable weaving uses a technique of supplementary warp threads that makes the pattern stand out. Natural dyes are still in use. In Bhutan three main types of looms exist: the pedal loom, backstrap loom, and card loom. Among them, the most common is the portable backstrap loom. The warp is attached to a fixed object in the house and loops around the back of the weaver. Tension on the warp is maintained by moving backward. This loom is found throughout Asia. Cotton, silk, wool, and yak hair are used to weave fabrics on backstrap looms for different types of uses, such as men's dress, women's dress, shoulder cloths, ceremonial cloths, bags, and so forth, in a great variety of intricate patterns. Its disadvantage is that it can produce only narrow bands of cloth. Thus, to produce a single *kira* or a blanket for one person requires three widths, which are sewn together.

Almost all of Bhutan's weavers are female. Over generations, the traditional designs for *gho* and *kira* have been passed on orally from mother to daughter and vary little. Stripes are usual and are worn vertically by men and horizontally by women. On heavier woolen clothing, checked patterns are common, and this design is worn by both men and women. The intricacy of design, the quality of the threads, the craftsmanship, and the cleanliness of a *gho* and *kira* reflect the status of a family.

Eastern Bhutan is well known for its stunning, hand-woven textiles.

LEISURE

Youths enjoying a game of soccer on a sandy field in Bhutan.

>THE GREAT MAJORITY OF BHUTANESE lead full working lives in the fields and pastures. Their farming methods are primitive, and the use of laborsaving devices is limited. Although there are good and bad harvests, the average family manages to produce sufficient food to meet its own needs, with a little surplus to bring in extra income.

Times of the year that are not labor-intensive are usually given over to house repair, weaving of cloth and baskets, and doing the many tasks

Movies in Thimphu attract large crowds, especially of young people.

Bhutanese have limited access to modern kinds of entertainment, and efforts to introduce infrastructure-intensive sports— where buildings are needed—such as bowling, have been met with dismal results. Bhutan has only one bowling alley, for example. Sports that can be played anywhere, such as tae kwon do (an unarmed martial art) and archery, seem to do better.

that are essential if the farm and family are to get by in the year ahead. It is during these times that couples, if they have decided to announce their union to the community, get married; young boys enter the monastery, with the whole village to see them off; and people accumulate merit by attending the temple, donating to the monks and the monastery, and sponsoring and attending *tsechu* festivities.

ARCHERY

Datse (DAT-say), or archery, Bhutan's national sport, is a high-profile activity. The country is well known for its level of skill in archery, and apart from the southern areas and monasteries, almost every village and *dzong* in the country has a place set aside for the activity. No festivity is complete without an archery match, and each match is accompanied by its cheerleading teams and high excitement.

Women follow the matches every bit as much as men. Dressed in their finest *kiras*, they cheer and encourage their team, dancing and singing before the competition and during intervals. They are not, however, included in competitive teams, although some all-women competitions are beginning to appear.

Believing that sleeping with a woman will drain the force, an archery team will sometimes sleep in a monastery or in a special accommodation at the *dzong* before the competition. They guard their equipment carefully, make offerings to the deities, and take special care that no woman touches a bow, which would take away its spring. A popular tournament involves two teams taking turns to shoot at wooden targets over a course of 360 feet (110 m).

Today many archers use high-tech imported bows, which are far more powerful and accurate than the traditional bamboo bows. Since the two types of bows cannot compete on equal terms, there are two separate tournaments each year—one for traditional bows and one for modern bows. It is now considered only a matter of time before Bhutan fields an Olympic medal-winning team. Bhutan's archery differs from Olympic standards in technical details such as the placement of the targets and the atmosphere. There are two targets placed over 328 feet (100 m) apart and teams shoot from one end of the field to the other. Each member of the team shoots two arrows per round. Traditional Bhutanese archery is a social event and competitions are organized between villages, towns, and amateur teams. There is usually plenty of food and drink, complete with singing and dancing. Attempts to distract an opponent include standing around the target and loudly making fun of the shooter's ability.

On June 30, 2002, Bhutan's national soccer team played against Montserrat, an island in the British West Indies, in a friendly match known jokingly as The Other Final, winning 4-0 at the Changlimithang Stadium in Thimphu. The match took place on the same day Brazil played Germany in the World Cup final— although at the time Bhutan and Montserrat were the world's two lowest ranked teams.

Bhutanese playing *tambola* (tumb-bo-lah), a popular game very similar to Western bingo.

FOOTBALL

Football of the British variety, or soccer, is played throughout the summer, usually in the evenings despite the monsoon rains. Competing teams often consist of older schoolboys. It is very much a local observer sport. Although Bhutanese soccer teams compete with neighboring countries, the sport is limited to towns and larger population centers and has yet to gain the enthusiastic following of archery.

THROWING STONES

Since archery is forbidden to monks, monasteries have invented their own alternative games and competitions. *Dego* (DEH-goh) is played with round, smooth stones. A small stick is stuck in the ground, and competitors take turns throwing their stones to land as close to the stick as possible. *Pundo* (PUN-do), similar to shot put, is played by monks and laymen. A large stone is thrown from the shoulder, and the longest throw wins.

MOVIES

There are five widely separated movie theaters in Bhutan—one in Thimphu, two in the border city of Phuntsholing, and one each in Samchi and Samdrup Jongkar. All of them show Hindi movies and Bollywood comedies very popular. In other parts of the country, films are shown in rented halls. Outside of urban centers, many Bhutanese have never seen a movie.

NIGHTCLUBS AND DRINKING PLACES

There are a few establishments in Thimphu and Paro that might be called nightclubs. They play loud music and offer little else. More common are small shops where men sit to drink Bhutan's wide variety of home-produced rum, gin, whiskey, brandy, and occasionally, cheap beer imported from India. Such shops usually double as *carom* parlors, an Indian game of flicking checker-like pieces enjoys immense popularity.

Bhutanese farmers believe three types of yeti exist. One is large, docile, and nonviolent. Another is a savage carnivore, 5 feet tall (1.5 m) with long hair and a Neanderthal appearance. The third yeti is small, shy, and shaggy-haired. All three leave their footprints at altitudes of 16,404 to 26,247 feet (5,000—8,000 m) and have a strong, pungent odor. Some scientists consider it possible that a species of mountain gorilla could survive in the remote heights, particularly if it had adapted its eating habits to what is available, notably yak meat, but none of the expeditions to track down a yeti has been successful. The yeti is pictured in old Bhutanese and Tibetan manuscripts and murals and has recently been honored in Bhutan by five designs of stamps bearing its image.

STORYTELLING

In the absence of a literary tradition outside of the sacred scriptures, the heroes and myths of Bhutan are kept alive for each new generation by dancers and storytellers. Storytelling is an amateur activity that takes place most often between generations of the same family. It also enlivens the education provided in the monasteries and in schools, since much Bhutanese history is indistinguishable from myth, particularly the exploits of Guru Rimpoche and Shabdrung Ngawang Namgyal, who followed the deity Yeshey Goenpo (who was in the form of a raven at the time) to find the way to Bhutan. Tibetan lama Ngawang Namgyal unified Bhutan, then supposedly spent 54 years meditating, though he was actually dead, during which time he is credited with repulsing attacks from Tibet and setting up an art and handicrafts school. Sometimes truth is stranger than fiction. The blue poppy was once dismissed as a myth by non-Bhutanese prior to its actual discovery by George Leigh Mallory in 1922. It remains rare, but photographs of the plant do exist. Another instance where myth and reality converge is the yeti, the abominable snowman. Bhutanese claim to have seen it, although foreign expeditions organized to track the snowman have been unsuccessful.

Today new sports are gaining in favor; basketball and tae kwon do in particular are very popular. Modern sports are encouraged along with safeguarding the older ones. While women can now participate in many sports, they more often are avid spectators.

FESTIVALS

Twirling dancers from Dramitse at Paro Dzong, performing the Dance of the Drum during a *tsechi* festival.

MOST IMPORTANT FESTIVALS and events in Bhutan are scheduled according to the Bhutanese calendar. A very few dates, commemorating significant events, are fixed on the Western calendar, such as Bhutan's National Day on December 17, which is the date the monarchy was established in 1907, and the crane festival, which celebrates the black-necked cranes on November 12.

Translating the Bhutanese calendar into the Western calendar is complicated, especially since finding the most auspicious time for an event is very important. Even after astrologers have intervened and local differences have been accounted for, it is still difficult to fix a date except in a broadband, which may be 2 to 4 weeks in the case of *tsechu* festivals and as much as 2 months for Losar, the New Year.

Fortunately, dates of festivals are now published on the Internet and are updated regularly as changes are made for one reason or another. An example of the Internet schedule for the year 2011 is given on page 119. The dates will not be the same in years to come.

Attendance by the public at any official festival, such as a *tsechu*, is not obligatory, but no one would want to be left out. Bhutanese working away from home during one of these important religious festivals will make every effort to return and participate among family and friends.

The few Bhutanese who do celebrate individual birthdays use the Western calendar. Otherwise everybody has a collective birthday on Losar (LOH-sar), which falls sometime between January and March. Bhutanese count the time in the mother's womb as part of the life cycle and count themselves a year old the moment they are born.

THE BHUTANESE CALENDAR

The Bhutanese calendar is based on the Tibetan calendar, which is in turn based on the Chinese calendar. The divergence between Tibet and Bhutan goes back to the 17th century when a Bhutanese scholar, Pema Karpo, devised a new way of reckoning the time. Tibet did not go along with the innovations.

Under the Pema Karpo system, which remains the official Bhutanese system, each month has 30 days. Years are named after 12 animals and 5 elements, each animal taking on a different element in rotation. For instance, 2000 was the year of the Iron Dragon; 1988 was the year of the Earth Dragon; 1976 was the year of the Fire Dragon; 1964 was the year of the Wood Dragon; and 1952 was the year of the Water Dragon. The year of the Iron Dragon will come around again in 2012. The year 2011 will be the Iron Rabbit.

The 12 animals, in consecutive order are—dragon, serpent, horse, sheep, monkey, hen, dog, pig, mouse, ox, tiger, and hare, or rabbit.

In each 30-day month some days are auspicious, namely full moon days and the fourth day, which was the day the Buddha set out his religious principles. Significant events are set for auspicious days, and astrologers are quite content to add or skip a day, or even a whole month for that matter, to make an event fall on a good day.

THE *TSECHU*

The *tsechu* is a festival held in each *dzong* and some monasteries, usually, but not necessarily, on the 10th day of the Bhutanese month. Every *tsechu* is dedicated to Guru Rimpoche, the Second Buddha, and includes dance-dramas that illustrate his life.

TSECHU SCHEDULES FOR 2011

Punakha Dromche—February 8 to 12, Punakha

Chorten Kora—February 18 and March 4, Tashiyangtse

Paro Tsechu—March 15 to 19, April 14 to 18, Paro

Ura Yakchoe—May 13 to 17, Bumthang

Kurjey Tsechu—July 10, Bumthang

Wangdi Tsechu—October 4 to 6, Wangdi

Tamshingphala Choepa—October 5 to 7, Bumthang

Thimphu Tsechu—October 6 to 8, Thimphu

Tangbi Mani—October 10 to 12, Bumthang

Jambay Lhakhang—November 10 to 14, Bumthang

Mongar Tsechu—December 1 to 4, Mongar

Tashigang Tsechu—December 2 to 5, Tashigang

Tongsa Tsechu—January 2 to 4, Tongsa

Lhuntse Tsechu—January 2 to 4, Lhuntse

Celebrated for 3 to 5 days, the heart of the festival is always the same —the performance of elaborately costumed religious dances known as *chham*, which depict episodes from Guru Rimpoche's life and moral stories from Bhutanese history and mythology. The religious basis of events still allows plenty of secular additions and trimmings. Folk dances, performed mostly by young women, present refreshing interludes between the set pieces, and *atsaras* (at-sar-ras), or clowns, openly mimic the more humorless of the monks in their ritualized dances.

Tsechu means "10th day," and celebrations are held then because Guru Rimpoche performed all of his magical miracles on the 10th of the month.

MOCKING RELIGION

The *atsaras* present a "rite of reversal," reinforcing the message of the formal drama by behaving in a way that normally would be unacceptable in Bhutanese society. Only an *atsara* in the circumstances of a *tsechu* can make fun of religion and its monks. The *atsara* perform at the *tsechus* in a deliberately outrageous way, wearing masks with long red noses, making innuendos, and telling jokes that ridicule. The entertainment extends outside the *dzong* with fairs and archery competitions, each team with its following of female cheerleaders. Secular songs and dances by both sexes provide informal opportunities for people to interact. Participants wear their finest clothes and jewelry, eat the best food, and drink plenty of alcohol. Everybody gains merit simply by attendance, although some are considered to gain a bit more because they are contributing to the cost. It is also a social opportunity to meet old friends and perhaps make some new ones from among those who live in distant villages. There is much drinking, some gambling, and a little flirting. Many marriages have their beginnings at the *tsechus*.

DROMCHE

Besides the *tsechus*, a few of the more important *dzongs*, such as Thimphu, Paro, and Punakha, will stage a second large festival called a *dromche* (DROM-chay). Similar to a *tsechu*, these are dedicated to Yeshe Gompo (Mahakala) or Palden Lhamo, the two main protective deities of Drukpas. Not every *dzong* can sponsor a *dromche* every year. Probably the best-known and most spectacular *dromche* is that of Punakha, which always concludes with a grand procession that reenacts episodes from the war with Tibet in the 17th century.

Jesters—known as *atsaras*—at the traditional *tsechu* festival in Thimphu.

LOSAR

Gyalpo Losar, the Bhutanese New Year, should correspond to the new moon in February, although very often it does not. It is a secular festival with no great communal festivities to prepare, and there is no pragmatic need to fix the date before agreement has emerged on the most auspicious day for it. The result is that different parts of the country can celebrate at different times. It is a relatively quiet affair, with archery competitions similar to any holiday. For most people, Losar is a time for the family to come together, visit, worship the deity of choice or of the region, and eat and drink abundantly.

SECULAR FESTIVALS

In addition to Losar and local festivals peculiar to a region or an area, there are two important secular festivals where the national identity takes priority—National Day on December 17, which celebrates the beginning of the Wangchuck monarchy; and the King's Birthday on November 11. These are celebrated throughout the kingdom with parades and dances in which schoolchildren play the central roles.

The Jambay Lhakhang festival is one of the most important in Bhutan, and its highlights are the Mewang, or the fire ceremony, and the Tercham, a sacred naked dance held at midnight. The fire dance is held in the evening to bless infertile women so that they may bear children.

FOOD

Villagers and city folks bargain hunting together at the weekend market in Thimphu.

CHAPTER 13

BHUTAN IS RENOWN FOR THE beauty of its landscape, the friendliness and hospitality of its people, the magnificent architecture of its *dzongs*, and its ancient colorful festivities. Cuisine is not one of its national attractions. The fact that Bhutanese villagers got the inspiration for one of their staple dishes from an Englishman is perhaps noteworthy.

Bhutan imports 34 percent of its grain food needs.

Bhutanese in the Paro Valley dry homegrown chilies on rooftops. Vegetables are an integral part of the Bhutanese diet because of the nation's Buddhist lifeway, which precludes slaughter, and a lack of cold storage facilities.

This Englishman traveled in Bhutan in the 18th century and lived on a diet of boiled rice and potatoes; many farmers exist on pretty much the same daily lunch, to which the inescapable Bhutanese ingredient of chilies is added. Chilies were essentially the only seasoning until the 1950s, when garlic, onions, and ginger—which had been used daily throughout the rest of Asia for centuries—were introduced to Bhutan and very quickly spread their agreeable flavors throughout the kingdom.

PREPARATION

The average Bhutanese kitchen is as uncomplicated as the diet. Metal pots, a frying wok, a tripod to hold them above the flames—or, in its absence, some well-placed rocks—and a long machete-like knife to chop firewood gathered from the fallen debris of trees, and the cooking place is ready. The kitchen and its fire is normally inside the house, except in the south where it is attached to the main house. In towns and more accessible areas, wood-burning stoves are sometimes found. These are more economical of firewood, safer, and provide a more controlled heat. Like all imports from India, however, stoves are too expensive for the average Bhutanese household.

Stews are popular and easy to cook in a Bhutanese kitchen. Cheese is melted, vegetables and meat are, rarely, thrown in, and water is added to a level depending on the number of servings needed. Usually, but not always,

phagshaphu: *Next to* ema datse *(chilies in cheese sauce), this is the dish most likely to tempt a Bhutanese. Strips of dried pork fat are stewed with radishes or turnips and plenty of dried chilies.*

phagshaphintshom: *Pork in rice noodles.*

gondomaru: *Scrambled eggs cooked in butter.*

noshahuentsu: *Stewed pork with spinach.*

bjashamaru: *Chicken stewed in garlic and butter sauce.*

momos: *This Tibetan dish is found throughout the Himalayas. These small steamed dumplings are filled with meat or cheese.*

tsampa: *Another Tibetan dish, in which barley flour is mixed with salt and butter, kneaded into a paste and roasted.*

daal-baat: *Rice with lentils and side vegetables, some pickles, and curry—the basic meal of southerners and the Nepalese. It is available in hotels that cater to Indians and is quite popular as well with the central and northern Bhutanese who have tried it.*

the women of the family do the cooking. Stews are usually served and eaten in their cooking pots unless a special occasion calls for the distribution of plates.

STAPLES

The Bhutanese eat enormous amounts of rice and comparatively little else with it. There is a preference for red rice, although both red and white rice are often eaten together. Gradually, rice is becoming the main staple of most of the entire country. In villages situated at high altitudes, however, rice will not grow. Instead, local wheat and buckwheat are made into pancakes and noodles. Dried, crushed kernels of corn may be added to leftover curry and eaten as a breakfast porridge. Some barley and millet are also eaten, although this is less popular than rice. Rice is usually unpolished and thereby retains its vitamins and fiber. Potatoes are eaten often enough to merit inclusion as a staple, but they are treated as a vegetable and usually cooked in a stew.

When traveling or working long hours in the fields, farmers carry a covered basket of *zow* (zow), rice that is boiled and then fried.

MEAT AND FISH

Most dried meat and fish sold in the market comes from India, including beef. There are no slaughterhouses in Bhutan and few refrigerated storage centers. None of the trucks bringing meat and fish from India is refrigerated, which accounts for the preference for dried foods. Most of the yak meat and pork originate in Bhutan, and these animals are presumed to have met with an accident or died of old age. Jokesters say that considering how few vehicles there are in Bhutan, an extraordinary number of animals perish in car accidents.

Most daily stews contain a bone or two with some meat on them, enough to prevent the Bhutanese diet from being totally vegetarian and to impart some taste to the stew. On special occasions Bhutanese serve squares of pig fat. This appears to contain its own preservative and is said to be full of energy.

Typical food: red rice, potatoes with chilies, and asparagus. The Bhutanese enjoy most of their meals with *suja* (butter tea) or *ara* (a spirit distilled from rice, wheat, or corn).

VEGETABLES

Bhutanese grow and eat potatoes, mushrooms, asparagus, and some seasonal, green leafy vegetables. These are supplemented with food products collected along the paths and forests on the way to and from the fields—bamboo shoots, mushrooms, taro, yams, sweet potatoes, wild bananas, and river weeds. During the monsoon months, when forest foods are plentiful and delivery of Indian meat to remote areas is difficult because of rained-out roadways, the diet consists mainly of vegetables.

Chilies are considered to be a vegetable and are prepared as such. The national dish, *ema datse* (yee-mah-dat-say), is made entirely of hot, green chilies in a sauce of fresh melted cheese.

CHURPI

Churpi (choor-pi) is sold in the form of small yellow cubes. Made of yak milk, this smoked cheese is so hard it can be repeatedly hit with a hammer and still keep its small, rectangular shape. It is held in the mouth for hours, being moved around with the tongue rather than chewed. It never softens and only gradually dissolves away. Churpi has a distinctive taste. It gets the saliva flowing and is said to keep hunger at arm's length with zero calories.

SNACKS

Bhutanese do not eat dessert after a meal but make a variety of snack foods to present to guests or to sell in small shops. *Kabze*, or fritters, are sold at festivals. *Sip* are flattened rice cakes. *Gegasip* are flattened corn cakes. These are often dipped in sweet tea and eaten for breakfast. More fruit is now grown for export, and some of it finds its way into the diets of those who live at higher altitudes. Fruit is more likely to be eaten as a snack rather than incorporated into meals.

Milk is rarely drunk but is churned into butter and the buttermilk that is left behind is turned into a cheese much like cottage cheese. Small, soft cheeses are not eaten as snacks but are used in sauces. *Churpi*, a hard, dried, smoked yak cheese, on the other hand, is a popular between-meals plaything for the teeth.

DRINKS

Tea is widely consumed, and there are two popular kinds—*seudja*, which is tea churned with salt and butter, and *nadja*, Indian-style tea brewed with milk and sugar. Coffee is rarely drunk, even in towns. Next to tea and water,

Religious strictures against taking a life curtail variety in the cuisine, but few Bhutanese are fully vegetarian (vegan). This includes monks, who eat the same staple foods as any other Bhutanese.

A woman serving her guest *ara*, a local spirit brewed from rice or corn that is popular with the rural population.

When offered food, one says *meshu meshu*, covering one's mouth with the hands in refusal, according to Bhutanese etiquette, and then gives in on the second or third offer.

alcohol is the most common drink. Alcoholic beverages that are made and sold in Bhutan span a full range—whiskey, gin, rum, vodka, and brandy. These lucrative products are also exported to other countries. Beer is imported from India and is sold at prices lower than in its country of origin. Regionally, hard cider is distilled from apples, and peach and apple brandies are also produced.

Drinking alcohol is widely incorporated into rituals and festivals, and the most common marriage ceremony is a simple exchange of glasses of wine.

PLAYING THE HOST

The host is obliged to offer a guest tea or alcohol. The guest must take at least a sip or lift the cup a couple of times to the lips, even if he or she does not drink it. A first refusal will simply be taken as good manners—meaning that the guest should not seem to pounce on the beverage—and the host is expected to make the offer again. The guest should ideally leave the drink until the host invites the guest with a small touch on the cup or saucer.

If a meal is to be served, alcoholic drinks with snacks will be served 1 or 2 hours ahead of the meal. Guests of high status visiting a humble family are likely to be received in the "chapel"—often the best room in the house, with the images of deities around—to reflect the elevated status of the guests. When dinner is served, the host may not eat with his guests but simply serves them. Immediately after the meal, the guest puts down his plate and leaves quickly. To hang around would be seen as bad manners.

INTRODUCING MODERN COOKING METHODS

In 2005 The Energy and Resources Institute (TERI) conducted an extensive survey to develop an Integrated Energy Management Master Plan (IEMMP) for the Royal Government of Bhutan. The study found that the residential sector accounts for the highest use (46.8 percent) of the total energy consumption in the country. Of the main residential sector end uses such as family cooking, lighting, space heating, and cooking fodder for cattle, family cooking alone accounts for 66 percent of the residential energy share, followed by fodder cooking. The majority of rural households in Bhutan use fuelwood for cooking.

As a result, the per capita fuelwood consumption in rural areas is a very high 1.19 tons per capita per year. To make fuelwood consumption sustainable, the government has regulated fuelwood use with each rural household in the country being allotted two standing trees per annum (each measuring approximately 35 inches or 90 cm in diameter) as fuel for household consumption. In spite of the regulation, the high consumption reportedly puts tremendous pressure on the forests with households often resorting to the unauthorized collection or purchases of fuel to meet their needs.

Traditional open-cooking stoves are very inefficient and consume a large amount of firewood every day. The Bhutanese government is trying to introduce LPG or electric stoves that are more environmentally friendly, considering that electrified households consume almost 23 percent less fuelwood compared with the unelectrified households. In fact, electricity tends to be the primary energy source for cooking once a household gets electrified. To reduce fuelwood consumption and to promote cleaner cooking, experts recommend that biomass-based turbo stoves or gasifier stoves, both more efficient wood-gas stoves, be introduced widely. Also, a wide-scale introduction of electric devices for cooking is projected in electrified areas.

EMA DATSE (CHILIES AND CHEESE SAUCE)

4 servings

3 ounces (85 g) cheddar cheese, grated

1 tablespoon (5 ml) flour

2 cups (500 ml) beef stock

1 medium onion, sliced

Garlic, several cloves, minced

3 green chilies, split, seeded
   and chopped

Salt to taste

1 tablespoon (15 ml) butter

- In a small bowl, mix the cheese with the flour.

- Bring the stock to a boil in a deep pot. Add the onion, garlic, and chilies and simmer until the vegetables are tender.

- Season with salt.

- Sprinkle half the cheese and flour mixture into the stock, and then cook for 1 minute or until the sauce thickens.

- Add the remaining cheese and flour mixture and the butter. Stir well, then cover and turn off the heat.

- Leave for 5 to 7 minutes, and then serve with plain steamed rice.

SWEET RED BEAN SOUP

4 servings

7 cups (1.75 L) water

1 cup (250 ml) dried red kidney beans, soaked in cold water overnight

⅓ cup (85 ml) dried lotus seeds, soaked in cold water overnight

⅓ to ½ (85 ml to 125ml) cup sugar

¼ cup (60 ml) pearl tapioca

¼ cup (60 ml) gluten rice balls

1 tablespoon (15 ml) vanilla

- Combine water and drained beans in a large pot. Bring to a boil.
- Reduce heat to simmer, cook uncovered until beans are tender (about 2 hours).
- Add lotus seeds and sugar, tapioca, and rice balls, cook until soup thickens a little and lotus seeds are tender but not mushy (about 20 minutes).
- Add vanilla.
- Serve hot for a perfect winter dessert, or let the soup cool and refrigerate for a cold soup.

Note for variation: Take out the beans, increase the amount of lotus seeds, and have a lotus seed sweet soup.

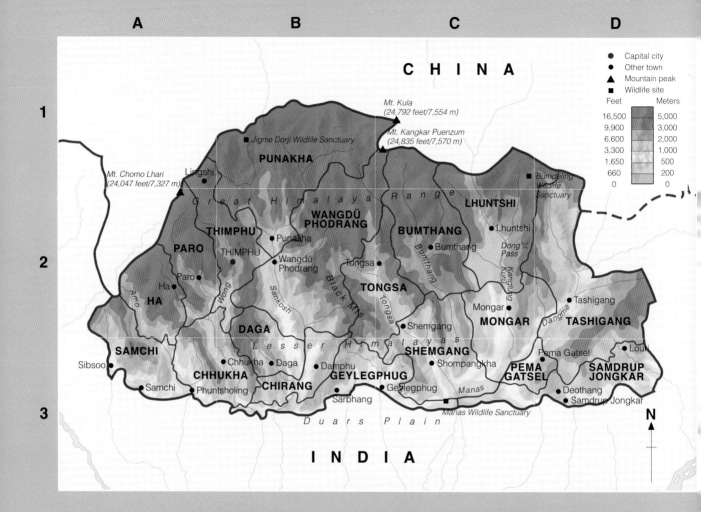

A   **B**   **C**   **D**

C H I N A

● Capital city
● Other town
▲ Mountain peak
■ Wildlife site

Feet		Meters
16,500		5,000
9,900		3,000
6,600		2,000
3,300		1,000
1,650		500
660		200
0		0

1

Mt. Kula
(24,792 feet/7,554 m)

Mt. Kangkar Puenzum
(24,835 feet/7,570 m)

■ *Jigme Dorji Wildlife Sanctuary*

PUNAKHA

Lingshi

Bumdeling Wildlife Sanctuary

Mt. Chomo Lhari
(24,047 feet/7,327 m)

Great Himalaya Range

WANGDÜ PHODRANG

LHUNTSHI

Lhuntshi ●

THIMPHU

BUMTHANG

PARO

Punakha ●

Bumthang ●

Bumthang

Dong Pass

2

THIMPHU ●

Wangdü Phodrang ●

Paro ●

Tongsa ●

Ha ●

TONGSA

Mongar ●

● Tashigang

HA

Amo

Wong

Sankosh

Black Mts.

Tongsa

MONGAR

TASHIGANG

Kanglung Kung

Dangme

DAGA

Lesser Himalayas

Shemgang ●

SAMCHI

SHEMGANG

Pema Gatsel ●

Loun ●

Sibsoo ●

● Chhukha

Daga ●

Shompangkha ●

SAMDRUP JONGKAR

● Damphu

GEYLEGPHUG

PEMA GATSEL

CHHUKHA

Samchi ●

● Phuntsholing

CHIRANG

Geylegphug ●

Manas

Deothang ●

Samdrup Jongkar ●

Sarbhang ●

■ *Manas Wildlife Sanctuary*

3

Duars Plain

N

I N D I A

MAP OF BHUTAN

ECONOMIC BHUTAN

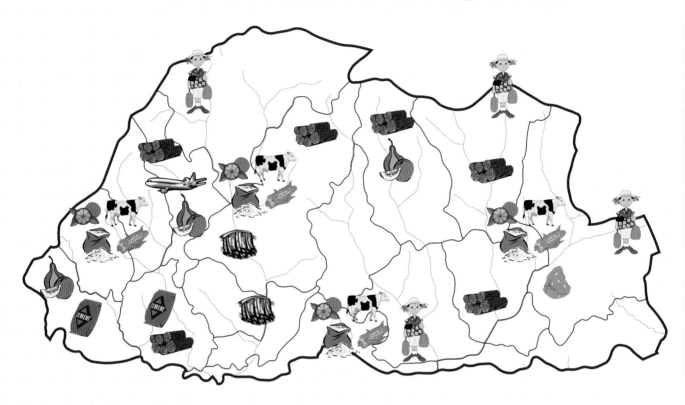

Agriculture

 Citrus

 Corn

 Livestock

 Rice

Manufacturing

 Cement

 Canned fruit

Natural Resources

 Gypsum

 Hydropower

 Timber

Services

 Airport

 Tourism

ABOUT THE ECONOMY

OVERVIEW

The economy of Bhutan, one of the world's smallest and least developed nations, is based on agriculture and forestry, which provide the main livelihood for more than 80 percent of the population. Agriculture consists largely of subsistence farming and animal husbandry. Rugged mountains dominate the terrain and make the building of roads and other infrastructure difficult and expensive. The economy is closely aligned with India's through longstanding trade and monetary links and dependence on India's financial assistance. The industrial sector is technologically backward, dominated by cottage industry-type production. Most development projects, such as road construction, rely on Indian migrant labor. Model education, social, and environmental programs are underway with support from multilateral development organizations. Each economic program takes into account the government's desire to protect the country's environment and cultural traditions.

GROSS DOMESTIC PRODUCT (GDP)
$3.257 billion (2009 estimate)

CURRENCY
Ngultrum (Nu).
US$1=Nu 44.3536 (2010 estimate)

GDP GROWTH
5.7 percent (2009 estimate)

NATURAL RESOURCES
Timber, hydropower, gypsum, calcium carbonate

AGRICULTURAL PRODUCTS
Rice, corn, root crops, citrus, food grains, dairy products, eggs

MAJOR EXPORTS
Electricity (to India), cement, copper wire, manganese, vegetable oil, fruit, cardamom, gypsum, timber, precious stones, spices, handicrafts

MAJOR IMPORTS
Fuel and lubricants, grain, passenger cars, machinery and parts, fabrics, rice

MAIN TRADE PARTNERS
India, Japan, Singapore, Bangladesh, Nepal

WORKFORCE
331,900 (2010 estimate)

UNEMPLOYMENT RATE
3.3 percent (2010 estimate)

INFLATION
8 percent (2008 estimate)

EXTERNAL DEBT
$347.1 billion (2009 estimate)

ANNUAL INCOME (PER CAPITA)
$1,321 (2006 estimate)

CULTURAL BHUTAN

Jigme Dorji National Park
This is the largest national park of Bhutan, covering 1,671 square miles (4,328 square km). It occupies almost the entire Gasa District, as well as the northwestern areas of Thimphu District and Paro District and spans all three climate zones of Bhutan. It is the country's most active geothermic region.

Punakha
Punakha was the seat of the government and administrative center of Bhutan until 1955, when the capital was moved to Thimphu. The *dzong*, situated at the confluence of two rivers, is one of the most spectacular in the country.

Wangdü Phodrang
The road from there to Tongsa is one of the prettiest in Bhutan, passing streams, forests, and villages before climbing the Pelela Pass on the Black Mountain range into the Tongsa Valley. The formidable *dzong* on top of the hill is the town's most visible feature. This is the last town on the highway before entering central Bhutan.

Tongsa
Tongsa, in the center of Bhutan, used to be the seat of power for the Wangchuck dynasty. Built on a mountain spur high above the gorges of the Mangde Chhu, the *dzong* controlled east-west trade for centuries. The only road connecting eastern and western Bhutan passed through the courtyard of the *dzong*.

Bumdeling Wildlife Sanctuary
This sanctuary is located within the districts of Tashigang, Lhuntshi, and Mongar and shares a border with Tibet and India. Over 100 species of mammals are found here alongside 130 species of butterflies. This is also home to Dechenphodrang Lhaghang, one of the most handsome monasteries in Bhutan.

Thimphu
Bhutan's capital, is situated in the beautiful Wang Chuu Valley and is draped over altitudes of 7,375 feet (2,248 m) to 8,688 feet (2,649 m) above sea level. It contains most of the important political buildings in Bhutan, including the National Assembly and Dechencholing Palace, the residence of the king.

TrumshingLa National Park
This park was created in 1998 and is the newest in Bhutan. The altitudes in the park range from less than 3,281 feet (1,000 m) above sea level to over 13,123 feet (4,000 m). In 2000 the World Wildlife Federation captured the image of a tiger at 9,843 feet (3,000 m) above sea level here.

Rinpung Dzong
This is a large Drukpa Kagyu Buddhist monastery and fortress in Paro District, with 14 shrines and chapels. It houses the district Monastic Body and government administrative offices of Paro Dzongkhag.

Phajoding Monastery
Located at 11,975 feet (3,650 m) above sea level, about a 3-hour walk from the capital, Thimphu. The monastery was founded in 1224 by Phajo Drugom Zhigpo, the Tibetan lama who spread the Drukpa Kagyud sect of Buddhism in Bhutan. Visitors are rewarded with a stunning view of Thimphu.

Tashichho Dzong
This *dzong* is the most prominent landmark in Thimphu. It is a Buddhist monastery and fortress. It has been the seat of Bhutan's government since 1955 and presently houses the throne room and offices of the king.

Jigme Singye Wangchuck National Park
This is the second-largest protected area of Bhutan, sprawling across 502 square miles (1,300 square km). The eastern part of the park shelters 20 percent of Bhutan's highly endangered tiger population. Other endangered species in the park include the musk deer, Himalayan black bear, golden langur, clouded leopard, and red panda.

Royal Manas National Park
The Royal Manas National Park is home to tigers, leopards, rhinos, and elephants as well as more than 360 bird species. It covers over 395 square miles (1,023 square km) and 92 percent of the park is still forested. This unique park is one of the best examples of the Eastern Himalayan ecosystem.

ABOUT THE CULTURE

OFFICIAL NAME
Kingdom of Bhutan

FLAG DESCRIPTION
Centered along the dividing line of this yellow and orange flag is a large black and white dragon facing away from the hoist side. The dragon, or *Druk* (Thunder Dragon), is the emblem of the nation. Its white color stands for purity and the jewels in its claws symbolize wealth. The background colors represent the spiritual and secular powers within Bhutan. The orange is associated with Buddhism, whereas the yellow denotes the ruling Wangchuck dynasty.

TOTAL AREA
13,285 square miles (38,394 square km)

CAPITAL
Thimphu

MAJOR RIVERS
Manas, Sankosh, Bumthang, Drangme Chhu

HIGHEST MOUNTAIN PEAK
Kangkar Puenzum (24,835 feet/7,570 m)

CLIMATE
Tropical in southern plains; cool winters and hot summers in central valleys; severe winters and cool summers in Himalayas

POPULATION
Approximately 750,000 (2010 estimate)

ETHNIC GROUPS
Ngalongs 50 percent, ethnic Nepalese 35 percent (includes Lhotshampas—one of several Nepalese ethnic groups), indigenous or migrant tribes 15 percent (includes the Sharchops)

RELIGION
Buddhism 75 percent (including Bon), Indian- and Nepalese-influenced Hinduism 22 percent, Christianity 2 percent, other 1 percent

BIRTHRATE
20 births/1,000 Bhutanese (2010 estimate)

DEATH RATE
7.4 deaths/1,000 population (2010 estimate)

AGE STRUCTURE
0 to 14 years: 30.2 percent
15 to 64 years: 64.3 percent
65 years and over: 5.5 percent (2010 estimate)

MAIN LANGUAGES
Dzongkha (official), Bumthangkha, various Tibetan dialects such as Ngalopkha and Sharchopkha, various Nepalese dialects, English

TIME LINE

IN BHUTAN	IN THE WORLD
2000 B.C.	
Nomadic herders inhabit the area.	
A.D. 627–649	**A.D. 600**
Introduction of Buddhism in Bhutan occurred during the reign of Tibetan king Srongtsen Gampo. He converted to Buddhism and ordered the construction of two Buddhist temples, at Bumthang in central Bhutan and at Kyichu in the Paro Valley.	Height of Mayan civilization.
700–800	**800**
Taktsang monastery founded by Tantric master Padmasambhava, often described as "another Buddha" or the "Second Buddha."	The Gregorian calendar terms B.C. (Before Christ) and A.D. (*Anno Domini*, or In the year of our Lord, meaning after the death of Jesus) adopted.
800	
Ninth-century monks call Bhutan "the hidden world." Civil wars throughout the century.	
842	**1000**
A Tibetan king's assassination led to many Tibetans fleeing to Bhutan.	The Chinese perfect gunpowder and begin to use it in warfare.
12th century	
The first fortresses known as *dzongs* built.	
1222	**1206–1368**
Tibetan Phajo Drugom Shigpo brings the Drukpa Buddhist teachings to the area.	Genghis Khan unifies the Mongols and starts his conquest of the world. At its height, the Mongol Empire under Kublai Khan stretches from China to Persia and parts of Europe and Russia.
1600s	
Tibetan lama Ngawang Namgyal unifies Bhutan.	
1627	**1620**
The first Westerners arrive in Bhutan—two Portuguese Jesuit priests.	Pilgrims sail the *Mayflower* to North America.
1656	
Full unification of central and eastern Bhutan. Country named Druk Yul, Land of the Thunder Dragon.	
1774	
Bhutan and the East India Company sign a treaty of cooperation.	**1775–1783**
	American Revolution
1841	**1789–1799**
British annex the Bhutanese-controlled Assam Duars.	The French Revolution.
1864–1865	**1861–1865**
British forces occupy southern Bhutan in the Duars War.	The U.S. Civil War.
	1869
	The Suez Canal is opened.

IN BHUTAN	IN THE WORLD
1885	
Ugyen Wangchuck brings Bhutan under one rule.	
1904	
Ugyen Wangchuck cooperates with British troops in invasion of Tibet.	
1907	
Ugyen Wangchuck is crowned as the first hereditary ruler, the Dragon King.	
1910	**1914**
Treaty signed with British giving them control over Bhutan's foreign relations.	World War I begins.
1926	**1939**
Ugyen Wangchuck's son Jigme Wangchuck becomes king.	World War II begins.
1949	**1949**
Treaty signed with newly independent India guaranteeing noninterference in Bhutan's internal affairs, but accepting Delhi's influence over foreign relations.	The North Atlantic Treaty Organization (NATO) is formed.
1952	**1950–1953**
Reformist monarch Jigme Dorji Wangchuck succeeds to throne as third king.	Korean War.
1953	
National Assembly established.	
1959	**1959–1975**
Several thousand refugees given asylum in Bhutan after Chinese annex Tibet.	Vietnam War.
1964	**1963**
Prime Minister Lhendup Dorji killed in dispute among competing political factions.	Assassination of U.S. President John F. Kennedy.
1968	**1997**
Jigme Dorji Wangchuck establishes the High Court.	Hong Kong is returned to China.
2003	**2003**
Assamese guerrillas, who had set up bases in southern Bhutan, flushed out by Bhutan.	War in Iraq begins.
2005	
The fourth king, Jigme Singye Wangchuck, announces general elections to be held in 2008, and that he will abdicate.	
2008	
His son, Jigme Khesar Namgyel Wangchuck, is crowned. He supervises transforming Bhutan into a constitutional democracy.	

GLOSSARY

atsara (AT-sar-ra)
A clown at *tsechu* festivals.

bodhisattvas (bod-hi-sat-vahs)
Enlightened Buddhist beings who choose to be reborn rather than entering Nirvana, in order to help others.

chham (CHARM)
Classical lama dancing.

Chhokey (Cho-kay)
Classical Tibetan language.

chorten (CHOR-ten)
A stupa, Buddhist funerary shrine or monument.

datse (DAT-say)
Archery.

dromche (DROM-chay)
A *tsechu* festival dedicated to Drukpa protective deities.

Drukpa (Drook-pah)
Official religious sect of Bhutan and the people of the sect.

Druk Yul (Drook-yool)
Land of the Thunder Dragon.

Duars (DOO-ars)
Eighteen valleys leading into Bhutan from the Indian plains.

dzong (DZONG)
A multipurpose fortress, monastary, and shelter.

gho (GOH)
Traditional male costume.

kira (KI-rah)
Traditional female costume.

kye tsi (kai-et-si)
Lifelong horoscope, based on a child's date of birth.

la (LAR)
A mountain pass; also a particle at the end of phrases or sentences to show respect.

Lhotshampas (Lhot-sharm-pahs)
Southerners of Nepali origin.

Losar (Loh-sar)
Bhutanese New Year.

Ngalongs (Ngar-longs)
Early migrants from Tibet.

Sharchops (Shar-khops)
Original people of the east.

tantras
Buddhist texts written in the 3rd to 10th centuries.

thangka (TANG-kha)
A religious painting.

tsechus (JHE-choos)
Festivals celebrating the history, myth, and morality of Bhutan.

FOR FURTHER INFORMATION

BOOKS

Berthold, J. *Bhutan: Land of the Thunder Dragon.* Somerville, MA: Wisdom Publications, 2005.

Brown, L., M. Bradley, S. Armington, R. Whitecross. *Bhutan* (Country Guide). 3rd ed. Oakland, CA: Lonely Planet, 2007.

Carpenter, R., and B. Carpenter. *The Blessings of Bhutan* (A Latitude 20 Book). Honolulu, HI: University of Hawaii Press, Illustrated Edition, 2002.

Das, B. *A Year in the Bhutan Himalaya.* Toronto, ON: Dundurn Press, 2007.

Pommaret, F. *Bhutan: Himalayan Mountain Kingdom* (Odyssey Guide). 6th ed. Sheung Wan, Hong Kong: Odyssey Publications Ltd., 2009.

Ricard, M. *Bhutan: The Land of Serenity.* London: Thames & Hudson, 2009.

Wangchuck, D. W. *Treasures of the Thunder Dragon: A Portrait of Bhutan.* Toronto, ON: Penguin Global, 2007.

FILMS

Bhutan—Gross National Happiness, CustomFlix, 2006.

Vendetti, T. *Bhutan: Taking the Middle Path to Happiness.* Vendetti Productions, 2007.

MUSIC

Drukpa, J. *Endless Songs from Bhutan,* Norway Music, 2000.

Various Artists. *Tibetan & Bhutanese Folk Music*, Vol. 4. Lyrichord Discs Inc., 1994.

Various Artists. *Tibetan Buddhist Rites from the Monasteries of Bhutan*, Vol. 1. *Rituals of the Drukpa Order.* Lyrichord Discs Inc., 1993.

BIBLIOGRAPHY

BOOKS

Aris, M. *Bhutan: The Early History of a Himalayan Kingdom*. Warminster, UK: Serindia, 1979.

Armington, S. *Bhutan*. Oakland, CA: Lonely Planet, 1998.

Berthold, J. *Bhutan: Land of the Thunder Dragon*. Somerville, MA: Wisdom Publications, 2005.

Brown, L., M. Bradley, S. Armington, and R. Whitecross. *Bhutan* (Country Guide). 3rd ed. Oakland, CA: Lonely Planet, 2007.

Das, B. *A Year in the Bhutan Himalaya*. Toronto, ON: Dundurn Press, 2007.

Kuensel (English and Nepali language newspaper). Thimphu, Bhutan.

Pommaret, F. *Bhutan: Himalayan Mountain Kingdom* (Odyssey Guide). 6th ed. Sheung Wan, Hong Kong: Odyssey Publications, 2009.

———. *An Illustrated Guide to Bhutan: Buddhist Fort of the Himalayas*. Hong Kong: The Guidebook Co. Ltd., 1990.

Ricard, M. *Bhutan: The Land of Serenity*. London: Thames & Hudson, 2009.

Zeppa, J. *Beyond the Sky and the Earth: A Journey into Bhutan*. Toronto, ON: Riverhead Trade, 2000.

WEBSITES

Bhote Culture. www.mnsu.edu/emuseum/cultural/oldworld/asia/bhoteculture.html

Bhutan Economic Statistics—Economy Watch. www.economywatch.com/economic-statistics/country/Bhutan/

Business Bhutan. www.businessbhutan.bt/

CIA World Factbook: Bhutan. https://www.cia.gov/library/publications/the-world-factbook/geos/bt.html

Himalayan Kingdom of Bhutan, The. www.tashidelek.com

Kuensel Online—Bhutan's Daily Newsline. www.kuenselonline.com/

Tourism Council of Bhutan. www.tourism.gov.bt/

UN Data Country Profile—Bhutan. http://www.un.org/esa/population/publications/countryprofile/

United Nations World Food Programme—Bhutan. www.wfp.org/countries/bhutan

U.S. Department of State—Bhutan. www.state.gov/r/pa/ei/bgn/35839.htm

INDEX

143

INDEX